SEO

2014 And Beyond

Search engine optimization will never be the same again!

By Dr. Andy Williams

ezSEONews
Creating Fat Content

Version 2.0.

Released: 6th December 2013

D1308285

What people said about "SEO 2013 & Beyond"

"Read this book and anything else you can get your hands on by this guy."

"Dr. Andy Williams is to my mind the man to listen to when it comes to the subject of building a website in a clean ethical manner. His explanations of what Google and the other search engines consider as part of the ranking process cannot be bettered. If you wish to create a long lived website that does not need to fear the latest Google update(s) then pay heed." **Jim**

"After 10 years online building and promoting websites, I became quite adept at SEO (both on-page and off), but that was then, and this is now! Having read this eBook from cover to cover, I think you would be hard pressed to find more informative, descriptive, and easy-to-understand material on the subject of present day SEO anywhere." **Andy Aitch**

"This is the right way to build websites. There is a slot of rubbish written by many so-called experts, but this is not one of them. If you want to learn the best way to do SEO, then this is the leading book I have read, and I have read many." **Dobsy "Dobsy" (UK)**

"Basically I loved this book and highly recommend it. It is the best couple bucks you will ever spend. It is easy to read, succinct, and brilliant. He offers a lot of great tips without all the fluff that some authors throw in to add page count. Thanks Andy for a good read that upped my

SEO IQ." **Nicole Bernd**

"Since Penguin was released in April 2012, SEO has been turned on its head. Creating themed content with LSI in mind, instead of keyword focused content, is now the way to go.

Amazingly, this is exactly what Andy has been teaching for the past ten years. I only wished I had known him when I started out in internet marketing as his style of teaching is the best. He's a very genuine and generous person and if you've been hit by Panda or Penguin, this book is exactly what you need." **Carole**

"Great book, super helpful and makes seo easy to understand, especially for ecommerce novice! Would definitely recommend to anyone trying to get a handle on best practices in seo." **cswaff**

"He was warning of a Panda type hit at least two years before the Panda was born. Although the Penguin has changed things more than a bit, in this book, Dr Andy clearly, and in simple terminology, explains the strategies and tactics needed to stay on the good side of Google." **Tony Crofts**

"Great at teaching the difference in old SEO practices vs. New techniques." **Ms. WriterGirl**

"Andy is one of the few people that I listen to when it comes to SEO because rather than "follow the usual crowd", that tends to share rehashed information with little value that's based on fact, he does his own testing to determine what is actually working for him, and then shares his own results." **J. Stewart**

"This book was a very quick and easy read from start to finish. I found it to be an excellent work with some very mature insight into the nuances of how to get in good graces with Google. It took a few of my beliefs and approaches to Search Engine Optimization and turned them upside down." **Jonathan W. Walker**

"This is ground breaking Internet marketing information. Stuff you won't find elsewhere. Being a longtime pupil of Dr. Andy, I have put much of it to the test myself and I know it proves out. If you are in the Internet business, you need to read this book." **Norman Morrison**

"After following Andy Williams for over 8 years now I had a hunch his new SEO, 2013 & Beyond would be a winner . . . and it is. Simple, straight forward and on target with respect to the latest updates, upgrades, and algorithmic mods by our friends at Google. Do what Andy teaches, especially with reference to great content creation, and you will be successful in your SEO efforts." **Chris Cobb**

Contents

DISCLAIMER AND TERMS OF USE AGREEMENT

The author and publisher of this eBook and the accompanying materials have used their best efforts in preparing this eBook. The author and publisher make no representation or warranties with respect to the accuracy, applicability, fitness, or completeness of the contents of this eBook. The information contained in this eBook is strictly for educational purposes. Therefore, if you wish to apply ideas contained within this eBook, you are taking full responsibility for your actions. The author and publisher disclaim any warranties (express or implied), merchantability, or fitness for any particular purpose. The author and publisher shall in no event be held liable to any party for any direct, indirect, punitive, special, incidental or other consequential damages arising directly or indirectly from any use of this material, which is provided "as is", and without warranties. The author and publisher do not warrant the performance, effectiveness or applicability of any sites listed or linked to in this eBook. All links are for information purposes only and are not warranted for content, accuracy or any other implied or explicit purpose. The author and publisher of this book are not in any way associated with Google. This eBook is © copyrighted by Lunasoft Marketing, SL and is protected under the US Copyright Act of 1976 and all other applicable international, federal, state and local laws, with ALL rights reserved. No part of this may be copied, or changed in any format, sold, or used in any way other than what is outlined within this eBook under any circumstances without express permission from Lunasoft Marketing, SL

Pre & post Penguin SEO

On February 11th, 2011, Google released the Panda update. The update was designed to filter out low quality web pages from the index. This was necessary because an earlier release (codenamed caffeine) massively increased the number of web pages that Google needed to handle - much of which was low quality. At the time, Panda left webmasters scratching their heads as to why their sites were penalized. The answer was simple – their pages were not deemed sufficient quality.

On 24th April 2012, Google unleashed the Penguin. If Panda was a 1 on the Richter scale of updates, Penguin was surely a 10. It completely changed the way we needed to think about SEO. It seems that Penguin's job was to find web pages that had been optimized beyond the "tolerance level" for that site, and punish them accordingly. That's right, just about everything you have been taught about SEO in the last 10 years can be thrown out the Window. Google has moved the goal posts.

On 22nd May 2013, Google unleashed Penguin 2.0 which went far deeper than the original Penguin algorithm. This was not just a data refresh, but a major update to Penguin itself, and it's only going to get tougher.

On 26th September 2013 Google announced yet another update, called Hummingbird. This update had actually rolled out around the 20th August 2013, but this one is less likely to have caused you problems than Panda or Penguin. We'll look at Hummingbird a little later.

Fast-forward to today...

Ask a bunch of webmasters to define the term SEO and I bet you'll get a lot of different answers. I'm sure that three of the most common phrases you'll hear are on-page factors, off-page factors, and link building.

Definitions of SEO will differ depending on the type of person you ask and even when you ask them. SEO before Google introduced the Panda update was easy. After the Panda update it was still relatively easy, but you needed to make sure your content was good. After Google released the Penguin update, SEO suddenly became a whole lot harder. Let me explain this with a diagram:

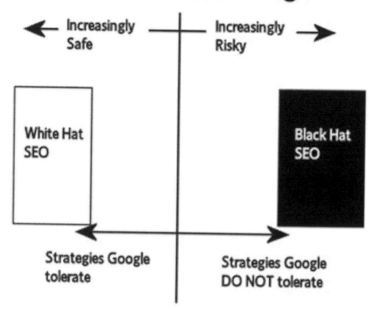

In the diagram above, I have noted two forms of SEO:

1. **White Hat SEO** – approved strategies for getting your page to rank well. Google offers guidelines to webmasters which spell out approved SEO strategies.

2. **Black Hat SEO** – strategies that Google dislike and would like to penalize. These include a whole host of strategies from on-page keyword stuffing to backlinking blasts using software to generate tens of thousands of backlinks to your site.

If you think of this as a sliding scale from totally safe "White Hat" SEO to totally dangerous "Black Hat" SEO, then you can imagine that as you move to the right with your SEO, you are more likely to get into hot water with Google (at least in the long term). As you move more to the left with your SEO, you are more likely to be safer with Google.

Before Panda & Penguin, most webmasters knew where the lines were drawn and took their risks accordingly.

When Google introduced Panda, the only real change to this was that webmasters now needed to make sure that the content on their website was unique, interesting to visitors, AND added something that maybe no other webpage on the topic had. No small task, but to beat Panda, which is essentially a Google add-on that looks for quality, this is our target.

When Google introduced Penguin, they completely changed the face of SEO, probably forever, or at least as long as Google continues to be the dominant search engine. Here is a diagrammatic representation of how I now see SEO:

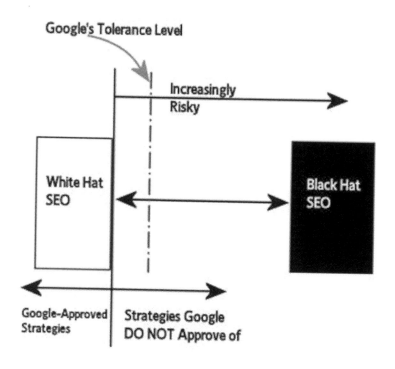

We've still got White Hat and Black Hat, but the connection between them is not as straight forward for the webmaster.

The "increasingly risky, increasingly safe" line that I drew in the first diagram (pre-Panda & Penguin) has now become the line that marks the approved and non-approved strategies boundary. This is now right up against the white hat boundary.

You'll notice that there is a new "Tolerance" lines drawn on the diagram. This tolerance line can move left to right, depending on how Google tweak their algorithm. If they want to come down hard on "spammers", they'll move the line to the left. If too many good sites get taken out as "collateral damage", they may move the tolerance line to the right a bit (although see the section later on "Trust v No-Trust"). Generally though, for most sites, the tolerance level is very close to the White hat boundary.

A webmaster that uses techniques which are further to the right than this approval line is risking their rankings.

Although these diagrams are good to work from, they do not display the whole truth.

Let's just consider the current state of SEO – the one post-Panda & Penguin.

Trust Vs no-trust

The Google Tolerance line will be in a different place depending on the site that is being ranked. For a site that has proven its worth and Google trusts a lot, we might see the diagram like this:

A trusted site

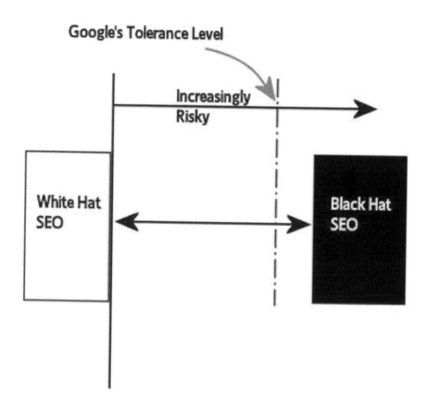

Yet for a new site, and one that has no track record to speak of, the diagram will probably look a lot more like this.

A non-trusted site

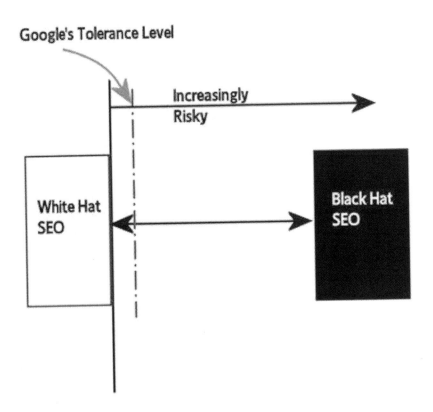

The only difference is in the location of the dashed "tolerance line".

In other words, Google are a lot more tolerant to sites that have built up authority and trust than they are to new sites, or sites that have not been able to attain a decent level of authority.

A high authority site with lots of trust can withstand a certain amount of spammy SEO without incurring a penalty (see later when we discuss "negative SEO"). The more authority, the more it can endure.

A new site on the other hand, would be quickly penalized for even a small amount of spammy SEO.

Webmasters living in the past

A lot of webmasters (or SEO companies vying for your business) may disagree with my take on modern-day SEO, and that's fine. The more people who just don't get it, the less competition there is for me and my clients.

I am sure you can find people that will say this is all rubbish and that they can get your pages ranked for your search terms (depending on the severity of competition of course), by heavily backlinking the page using keyword rich anchor text.

The process they'll describe is something like this:

1. Keyword research to find high demand, low competition phrases.
2. Create a page that is optimized for that keyword phrase.
3. Get lots of backlinks using that keyword phrase as anchor text.
4. Watch your page rise up the search engine results pages (SERPs).

If you don't care about your business, let them try. You might get short term gains, but you'll run the risk of losing all your rankings further down the line when Google catch up with you (and catch up they will... eventually).

To lose all of your rankings does not necessarily take a human review, though that can get your site penalized as well. No, getting your site penalized is far easier and the process Google has created is far more "automated" since the introduction of Panda and Penguin. Go over the threshold levels of what is acceptable, and the penalty is algorithmically determined and applied.

The good news is that algorithmic penalties can just as easily be lifted by removing the offending SEO and cleaning up your site. However, if that offending SEO includes low quality backlinks to your site (especially to the homepage), things are a little trickier.

Remember that SEO expert you hired that threw tens of thousands of backlinks at your site using his secret software? How can you get those backlinks removed? In many cases you can't, and moving the site to a new domain may be your only option.

In the rest of this book, I want to focus on what you need to do to help your pages rank better. I'll be focusing on purely white-hat strategies because black-hat is just not a long-term strategy. Remember, with the flick of a switch Google can change the goal posts again, leaving you out in the cold. Is it worth risking your business for short-term gains?

Before we go on to look at the 4 pillars of post-Penguin SEO, let's consider Hummingbird and where that fits into this puzzle.

Hummingbird - Another Animal in Google's Zoo

Hummingbird is the name given to Google's latest search algorithm (and completely replaces the old one). This is a major change to the way Google sorts through the information in its index and a change of this scale has probably not occurred for over a decade.

Think of it this way. Panda and Penguin were changes to parts of the old algorithm, whereas Hummingbird is a completely new algorithm, although it still uses components of the old algorithm.

The algorithm is basically the mathematical equation(s) used to determine the most relevant pages to return in the search results. The equation is built of over 200 components, things like PageRank and incoming links, etc.

Apparently the name Hummingbird was chosen because of how fast and accurate these birds are. Although a lot of webmasters won't agree, Google obviously assume that is what their search results are like.

Google wanted to introduce a major update to the algorithm because of the evolution in the way people use Google to search. An example Google have given is in "conversation search" where people can now speak into their mobile phone, tablet or even desktop browser to find information. Imagine you were interested in buying a Nexus 7 tablet. The old way of searching was to type something like this in the Google search box:

Buy Nexus 7

However, with speech, people have become a lot more

descriptive in what they are search for. For example, it's easy to just dictate into your search browser something like:

"Where can I buy a Nexus 7 near here?"

The old Google could not cope as well with this second search phrase, but the new Hummingbird is designed to do just that. The old Google would look for pages in the index that included some or all of the words in the search phrase. A page that included the exact phrase would have the best chance of appearing at the top of Google. If no pages were found with the exact phrase, then Google would look for pages that included the important words from that phrase, e.g. "where" "buy" and "nexus 7".

The idea behind Hummingbird is that it should be able to interpret what the searcher is really looking for. In this case, they are clearly looking for somewhere near their current location that they can purchase a Nexus 7.

In other words, Hummingbird is suppose to determine searcher intent and return pages that best match that intent (as opposed to best matching keywords in the search phrase). Hummingbird tries to understand exactly what the searcher wants, rather than just taking into account the words used in the search term.

Today, in 2014 and beyond, optimizing for specific keyword phrases has not just become difficult (because of Panda & Penguin), it has become less effective in driving traffic if those phrases do not match the intent of the searcher typing those phrases into Google.

The 4 pillars of post-Penguin SEO

I have been doing SEO for around 10 years now and I have always concentrated on long-term strategies. That's not to say I haven't dabbled in black hat, because I have. However, almost without exception, all of the sites I promoted with black hat SEO have now been penalized. Since I don't want you to suffer the same fate with your website, I'll only be discussing white hat, safe techniques here.

I divide SEO strategies into four main areas. These are:

1. Quality content
2. Site organization
3. Authority
4. What's in it for the visitor?

These are the four areas where you need to concentrate your efforts. So let's now have a look at each of them in turn.

1. Quality content

Before we begin, let me just say that a lot of SEO "experts" have disagreed with me on the need for quality content as a major ranking factor. They will often cite exceptions in the search engines where pages rank well for competitive terms without any on-page content. The fact that these exceptions rarely last more than a week or two escapes them. However, I do like to answer my critics. If you are one of those people that questions the need for quality content, then I encourage you to watch a video I recorded before you read the rest of this book. You can watch the video here:

http://bit.ly/1c6YTRZ

BTW; those that agree with me about the need for quality content, or those on the fence, can also watch that video. It's quite an eye opener.

So let's get back to the idea of quality content, and what that means.

There are a number of different types of content that you can add to your site including articles, product reviews, quizzes, videos etc. However, no matter what type of content you are looking at, it has to:

1. Be created for the visitor, not the search engines. That means it needs to read well and have no visible signs of keyword phrases that have only been added to help the Page Rank better.
2. Add value to the top 10 SERPs (if you want to rank in the top 10, your page has to be seen as adding something

unique to that collection of pages).

3. Give your visitors what they want.

To put it simply, all of the content on your site has to be the best you can make it.

A good rule of thumb I like to follow is this; would the content look out of place if it were published in a glossy magazine?

If you hire ghostwriters, make sure you proof read the content to ensure that any **facts are correct** and there are **no spelling or grammar errors**.

As you read through the content that you intend to post onto your website, ask yourself:

• Is it content that your visitors will find useful?

• Is there information in there that your visitors are unlikely to know, and therefore find informative?

• If it's a review, does it sound overly hyped up? Are both sides of the argument covered (i.e. positives and negatives)? Is there information in the review that is not available on the manufacturer's website or Amazon? Does the review offer a different way of looking at things which may help the buyer make a better informed decision prior to purchase?

To help us clarify what we see as quality content, let's take a look at some poor content.

Here is the first paragraph of an article I found online. Can you guess what **the** author was trying to optimize the page for?

Understanding Pomegranate Juice Benefits

Some people may not be that knowledgeable about pomegranate juice benefits but it is actually a very effective source of Vitamin C. The pomegranate fruit contains a lot of healthy nutrients and you can get a lot of good immune system boosters out of pomegranate juice benefits. It can actually provide around 16% of the required amount of Vitamin C that adults need to take on a daily basis. Pomegranate juice benefits also include Vitamin B5 as well as the antioxidant element of polyphenols and potassium.

The underlined keywords are part of the Kontera advertising system, so just ignore that.

It's not too difficult to guess the main phrase the author was targeting, is it?

"Pomegranate juice benefits" – it sticks out like a sore thumb. In fact, in a relatively short article (415 words) that phrase appeared 17 times. That's a density of 4%!

How many people think a density of 4% is OK or natural? Is repeating the same phrase 4 times every 100 words natural?

Let me tell you what a natural density is.

Ready for this....

It's **whatever density occurs naturally when an expert in their field writes an article.**

If you look back at that opening paragraph, there is an even bigger sin.

Here, look again:

Understanding Pomegranate Juice Benefits

Some people may not be that knowledgeable about pomegranate juice benefits but it is actually a very effective source of Vitamin C. The pomegranate fruit contains a lot of healthy nutrients and you can get a lot of good immune system boosters out of pomegranate juice benefits. It can actually provide around 16% of the required amount of Vitamin C that adults need to take on a daily basis. Pomegranate juice benefits also include Vitamin B5 as well as the antioxidant element of polyphenols and potassium.

Did you notice anything strange about that highlighted phrase?

It doesn't make sense, does it? This is a very clear indicator that the author was stuffing that phrase into the article in an attempt to help the article rank higher for that phrase.

You know, the sad thing is that this type of article may well have ranked well before Panda and Penguin. Why is that sad? Because web searchers had to put up with this kind of rubbish.

Today, no amount of sneaky black hat techniques could get this page into the top 10 (at least not for the long term). That is the difference between pre and post Panda/Penguin SEO.

If I actually do a search for "pomegranate juice benefits" in Google, the top ranked page (at the time of writing) included the exact phrase ONCE in an article of over 1000 words in length. That's a density of 0.1%.

OK, so the first lesson to learn – throw keyword density rules out of the window.

What may be a surprise to many, is that out of the top 10 pages ranking for the term "pomegranate juice benefits", only THREE have that phrase in the page title. In fact, **only three of the top 10** pages actually include that phrase anywhere in the article.

Perhaps you think that statistic is just a fluke?

Try it with any search term that isn't a brand name or product name. In general, the top 10 search results in Google list far fewer pages containing the actual search term (although this does seem to fluctuate somewhat as Google twiddle their algorithm "dials").

So just how is Google able to decide on how to rank webpages for the term "pomegranate juice benefits" (or any other search term), if they are not looking for that actual phrase in the content?

The answer to that lies in the words on the page. Let me ask you a question.

Does your article sound as if it was written by an expert?

The reason I ask is because when an article is written by somebody who really knows their subject, they will use a certain "niche vocabulary". That is, they will use words and phrases that actually define the topic of the article.

You can read an article I wrote on this called "Niche Vocabulary - why poor content can't hide in Google". You will see in that article, that if your content does not contain its niche vocabulary, you're very unlikely to rank in Google for the long term.

Every article you write will have its own niche vocabulary.

Two articles on a similar topic will share a percentage of that niche vocabulary, but not all of it will be shared.

Let's take the same example used in articles on epilepsy, and have a look at how the pages in Google use their niche vocabulary.

To carry out a test, I found a number of words on the top 10 pages of Google ranking for the term epilepsy using Web Content Studio. These words appeared on many of the top 10 pages ranking for that term. These are what I call theme words (or niche vocabulary), i.e. words that commonly appear in articles that are written on a given topic.

Here are the theme words I found for the term epilepsy:

age, aid, anti, brain, cause, children, control, develop, diagnosis, diet, doctor, drugs, epilepsy, epileptic, guide, health, help, home, information, ketogenic, life, living, log, medical, medications, part, plan, research, seizure, seizure-free, seizures, side, special, support, surgery, symptoms, take, term, test, time, treatment, types, unit, work

What I would like to do is check a couple of different epilepsy "sub-niches" to see if these words appear. The sub niches are:

1. Epilepsy treatment
2. Ketogenic diet

Both of these terms are highly related to epilepsy (the ketogenic diet is a diet that helps cure epilepsy in a number of patients). Since they are both talking about epilepsy, they both should contain a lot of the epilepsy niche vocabulary.

First let's have a look at the top ranking pages for the term **epilepsy.** Here is a screenshot showing the number one ranked article with the theme words I found earlier highlighted in yellow:

isturbed **brain** activity that **cause** changes in attention or behavior. se ses, incidence, and risk factors **epilepsy** occurs when permanent cha le **cause** the **brain** to be too excitable or jumpy. the **brain** sends out als. this results in repeated, unpredictable **seizures**. (a single **seizure** pen again is not **epilepsy**.) **epilepsy** may be due to a **medical** condit affects the **brain**, or the **cause** may be unknown (idiopathic). comm epsy include: stroke or transient ischemic attack (tia) dementia, such ase traumatic **brain** injury infections, including **brain** abscess, mening aids **brain** problems that are present at birth (congenital **brain** defec occurs during or near bith metabolism disorders that a child may be t henylketonuria) **brain** tumor abnormal blood vessels in the **brain** oth lage or destroy **brain** tissue **epilepsy seizures** usually begin betwee but they can happen at any **age**. there may be a family history of **seiz** epsy. **symptoms symptoms** vary from person to person. some peo le staring spells, while others have violent shaking and loss of alertnes **ure** depends on the **part of the brain** affected and **cause** of epileps the seizure is similar to the previous one. some people with epilen

You can only see a small section of the article here, as it's quite long, but I'm sure you'll agree that the theme words are well sprinkled throughout.

Let's repeat this but using the number one ranked article for the term **epilepsy treatment:**

with the introduction of dilantin (warner-lambert), has been a triumph of moder
ıe. the **development** of newer **medications, especially** tegretol (ciba-geigy) an
reckitt & colman) has meant that **epilepsy** can be suppressed in most patients
: serious or annoying **side** effects. this is not to say that every patient can be fully
lled, or that **side** effects do not occur. a continuing effort is being made by
ional pharmaceutical companies to find safer, more effective **treatment** ██
sy. new **drugs** are not cascading onto the market however, for the high cost of
ch, **development** and marketing (about a$150 million for any new drug) is an
ınt disincentive. how do **drugs** prevent **seizures?** strange to say, most of the
used in treating **epilepsy** today were discovered to have **anti-epileptic** proper
ıce. we have used these **drugs** with great benefit for years without really knowi
ey **work.** however, a more systematic search for new **anti**epileptic██s is n
vay, based on **research** progress in understanding how neurones transmit
:s to each other, and our increasing knowledge of the structure and function of tl
ane which surrounds each neurone. the **messages** that one neurone sends to the
ıeditated by releasing neurotransmitter chemicals, can either excite the neurone
line, or can inhibit its electrical activity. the identification of gamaa-amino butyric

Once again we see the theme words sprinkled throughout the content as we would expect, since this article is also about epilepsy.

Let's now look at the final example, which is the **ketogenic diet:**

ketogenic diet was then gradually forgotten as new anticonvulsant medications developed. the ketogenic diet has recently been 'rediscovered' and is achieving increasingly widespread use. its modern day role as alternative management for cl with difficult-to-control epilepsy is currently being re-defined. the ketogenic die a 'fad' or a 'quack diet', but rather is an alternative medical treatment for childr difficult-to-control epilepsy. the ketogenic diet should only be used under the supervision of a physician and a dietician. background fasting to achieve control seizure was described in both the bible and during the middle ages, but it was o during the early 1920s that scientific papers first appeared describing the beneficia effects of prolonged fasting for children whose epilepsy could not be controlled few medications then available. these papers claimed that starvation, drinking onl for 10 to 20 or more days, could result in control seizure for prolonged peric time. during this era, when the metabolic effects of diabetes were also being studi was noted that the biochemical effects of fasting could be mimicked by eating a di

This too has the theme words for epilepsy sprinkled throughout.

Since all of these articles have epilepsy theme words sprinkled throughout them, they could all theoretically rank for the term epilepsy, but the most important thing is that Google will know the article is about epilepsy because they contain epilepsy-related words and phrases.

Each of these articles actually has **a slightly different set of theme words** which help to define what area of epilepsy they are discussing. We could show this by finding theme words specific to each of the three articles and we would see they were different (though there would be a core of epilepsy related words).

However, let's try something a little different. Let's look at a second test.

Test 2 - I found a number of "theme phrases" – 2, 3 & 4 word phrases that are common to the top 10 ranked pages

for the three terms – epilepsy treatment, ketogenic diet &
epilepsy.

I pooled all of these phrases together and then checked the
top three ranking pages for epilepsy, epilepsy treatment,
and the ketogenic diet.

If each article has a slightly different niche vocabulary,
then we should see different theme phrases being used in
each of the articles. Let's have a look at the epilepsy article
first:

have simple staring spells, while others have violent shaking and loss
ness. the type of seizure depends on the ████████████ affected
cause of epilepsy. most of the time, the seizure is similar to the previo
some people with epilepsy have a strange sensation (such as tingling,
ling an odor that isn't actually there, or emotional changes) before eac
tre. this is called an aura. for a detailed description of the symptoms
ciated with a specific type of seizure, see: absence (petit mal) seizure
ralized tonic-clonic (grand mal) seizure partial (focal) seizure signs an
the doctor will perform a physical exam, which will include a detailec
at the brain and nervous system. an eeg (electroencephalogram) will
one to check the electrical ████████████ people with epileps
often have abnormal electrical activity seen on this test. in some cases
est may show the area in the brain where the seizures start. the brain
appear normal after a seizure or between seizures. to diagnose
psy or plan for ████████████ you may need to wear an eeg
rdar for days or weeks while you go about your everyday life. you

The phrases are marked in blue.

Here is a list of theme phrases found in the epilepsy article:

activity in the brain

atkins diet
blood sugar

causes of epilepsy
epilepsy medication
epilepsy medications
epilepsy surgery
ketogenic diet
part of the brain
seizure medicines
temporal lobe
vagus nerve

Let's repeat the test using the top ranking article for epilepsy treatment:

▓▓▓▓▓▓ to treat epilepsy. once started on anti-epileptic medication never stop it unless advised to do so by a doctor. stopping medication on one's own is likely to produce a series of major seizures, a dangerous condition. back to ▓▓▓▓▓▓▓▓▓ which drug to use the choice of drug depends on: the type of epilepsy. some drugs such as epilim are activ in a wide range of seizures (tonic-clonic, absence attacks, etc.) while zarontin, for example, is active only against absence seizures. possible side effects. for example, dilantin tends to promote hair growth on the body an face, and should be avoided in women of dark complexion. dilantin also seems more likely to produce slowing of thought processes including memory than the newer anticonvulsant such as tegretol or epilim, which do not usually produce these symptoms. anticipation of pregnancy. all ▓▓▓ ▓▓▓▓▓▓ drugs carry a small risk to the unborn child. we will consider this

Here are the theme phrases on the top ranked page for epilepsy treatment:

adverse effects
aid for seizures
anticonvulsant drug
anticonvulsant drugs

anti-epileptic drug
anti-epileptic medications
anti-seizure medications
controlling seizures
epileptic control
epileptic seizures
ketogenic diet
seizure control
seizure medications
temporal lobe
treatment of epilepsy
treatments for epilepsy

And finally for the phrase "ketogenic diet", here are the theme phrases:

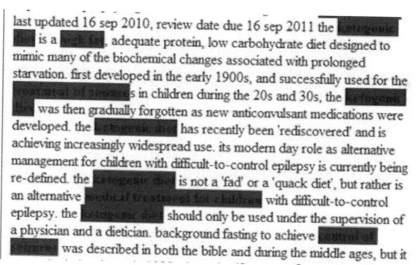

last updated 16 sep 2010, review date due 16 sep 2011 the ▮▮▮▮▮▮ ▮▮ is a ▮▮▮▮ ▮▮▮, adequate protein, low carbohydrate diet designed to mimic many of the biochemical changes associated with prolonged starvation. first developed in the early 1900s, and successfully used for the ▮▮▮▮▮▮ ▮▮ ▮▮▮▮▮▮s in children during the 20s and 30s, the ▮▮▮▮▮▮▮ ▮▮ was then gradually forgotten as new anticonvulsant medications were developed. the ▮▮▮▮▮▮▮ ▮▮▮ has recently been 'rediscovered' and is achieving increasingly widespread use. its modern day role as alternative management for children with difficult-to-control epilepsy is currently being re-defined. the ▮▮▮▮▮▮▮ ▮▮▮ is not a 'fad' or a 'quack diet', but rather is an alternative ▮▮▮▮▮▮ ▮▮▮▮▮▮▮▮ ▮▮▮ ▮▮▮▮▮▮▮ with difficult-to-control epilepsy. the ▮▮▮▮▮▮▮ ▮▮▮ should only be used under the supervision of a physician and a dietician. background fasting to achieve ▮▮▮▮▮▮ ▮▮ ▮▮▮▮▮▮▮ was described in both the bible and during the middle ages, but it

25

These are the phrases found:

anticonvulsant drug
anticonvulsant drugs
beta hydroxybutyric acid
body fat
control of seizures
control seizures
diet controls seizures
different anticonvulsants
high fat
high fat diet
high fat intake
medical treatment for children
protein and carbohydrate
seizure control
seizure type
treatment of seizure
while on the diet

Let's compare the theme phrases of these three articles in a table:

Epilepsy	Epilepsy Treatment	Ketogenic Diet
activity in the brain	adverse effects	anticonvulsant drug
atkins diet	aid for seizures	anticonvulsant drugs
blood sugar	anticonvulsant drug	beta hydroxybutyric acid
causes of epilepsy	anticonvulsant drugs	body fat
epilepsy medication	anti-epileptic drug	control of seizures
epilepsy medications	anti-epileptic medications	control seizures
epilepsy surgery	anti-seizure medications	diet controls seizures
ketogenic diet	controlling seizures	different anticonvulsants
part of the brain	epileptic control	high fat
seizure medicines	epileptic seizures	high fat diet
temporal lobe	ketogenic diet	high fat intake
vagus nerve	seizure control	medical treatment
	seizure medications	for children
	temporal lobe	protein and carbohydrate
	treatment of epilepsy	seizure control
	treatments for epilepsy	seizure type
		treatment of seizure
		while on the diet

This table clearly shows that each of the three articles have a different niche vocabulary.

As we saw above, all three articles have theme words relating to epilepsy as we would expect. However each of the articles also had their own set of theme phrases which help to distinguish the actual sub-niche within epilepsy.

The **epilepsy** article has a wide range of theme phrases relating to all aspects of epilepsy.

The **epilepsy treatment** article focused more on phrases that are related to the treatment of epilepsy (big surprise eh?).

The **ketogenic diet** article had more theme phrases relating to the diet itself and the control seizures.

How can you use this information to write better content?

If you are an expert in the field you are writing about, you will automatically and naturally use these theme words and phrases as you write about the topic. The truth is that you need to use these theme words and phrases if your article is to make sense and look authoritative.

If however you are not an expert, then things are a little more difficult. You need to find which words and phrases are important to the topic you want to write about.

As you write the content sprinkle in theme words (that are single words that are highly related to the niche). This will help the search engines to identify the topic. Also pick a small number of highly relevant theme phrases (2, 3 and 4+ word phrases) and include these in your content (once is enough but write for the visitor, so use theme words and phrases when you need to).

These theme phrases should be the most important ones that relate to the niche and will leave the search engines in no doubt about the topic. Do not under any circumstances use theme words or phrases that are not necessary. E.g. don't just repeat a phrase 3 or 4 times in the content because you want that page to rank for that term. Google's Penguin will be onto you and you could find your rankings drop for keyword stuffing or unnatural use of keywords.

Below is an example of a badly written article where theme phrases have been repeated solely for search engines. Here is the first half of an article. Ignoring the quality of the information in this piece, let's just look at an example of keyword stuffing:

DIY Architecture

Let's say you are planning a room addition. Did you know that you already possess the talents which allow you to calculate a comfortable size for the room addition? You may even possess some good design skills. Now you might think that I am wrong on this one.

For sake of discussion, let's assume that your local zoning ordinances will permit you to do just about anything. Some cities have strict setback lines and so forth that may limit the size of your planned addition - you must be aware of these limitations.

Go into your present living room. How does it feel? Imagine if it were say 6 feet wider and 8 feet longer. Maybe this size would allow you the space for that new couch, or a fireplace, built-in bookcases, whatever. The point is this. Use your existing rooms as starting points. You can measure them and stretch them to suit your needs. You need to start thinking in terms of space and how much you need.

Putting it on Paper

Remember earlier how I told you that my drafting skills were poor. Today, you don't need to know how to draw! If you have a fairly modern computer and sufficient memory, there are many affordable computer design programs that will draw your planned room addition.

I have highlighted one phrase that occurs three times (but I could have chosen a different example in this same article). The phrase is "room addition" and to me it sticks out because it is actually a little awkward to read, even unnatural when you read the text around the phrase (which is fluff and padding). When that happens, I assume that the webmaster included the term for the search engines, and if we check Google Keyword Tool, we can get a fairly strong confirmation of that:

	Save all	Search terms (1)			
Keyword		Competition	Global Monthly Searches ?	Approximate CPC (Search) ?	
room addition ▾		High	60,500	€2.67	

That phrase has 60,500 monthly searches, and costs advertisers around 2.67 Euros PER CLICK. With the AdSense ads on this site, that phrases could well have been a nice little earner.

Funnily enough, the site where this article is found used to be a site that Google showed off as a quality AdSense/Affiliate website. In the recent rounds of Panda and Penguin updates, this site was penalized. This caused a lot of webmasters to conclude that Google does not like affiliate sites. After all, an affiliate site that Google once showcased as a shining example was itself penalized.

My view on this is that Google simply does not like poor or spammy content. This particular site was probably lucky to get away with its content for as long as it did, and most probably never got a real in-depth human review. When Google introduced the Panda and Penguin updates, these largely automated pieces of code caught the site and identified much of its content as low quality and in violation of the Google guidelines. On looking through a lot of the earlier content on that site, I'd agree that it was penalized for good reason.

2. Site organization

A note about Exact Match Domain names

An exact match domain (EMD) is one that is basically using the main keyword phrase you are targeting as the domain name, e.g. buyviagraonline.com (if you wanted to target "buy Viagra online"). Typically, EMD websites target very few keywords, with all eggs being placed firmly in the "EMD phrase" basket.

If you are starting a new website, choosing a domain will be the first task you'll need to do. Many people who teach SEO will tell you to go for an EMD because it offers ranking advantages over non-EMDs. This was true in the past, but less so now. In fact, on September 28th 2012, Google released an update that was meant to reduce the ranking ability of poor quality EMDs. You can read the announcement by Matt Cutts (Google's head of spam) on Twitter here. This shouldn't really have come as a surprise to the better SEOs, because Matt Cutts announced that Google would be looking at why EMDs ranked so well when he spoke at Pubcon in November 2010 (2 years ago).

The problem with EMDs now is that they are scrutinized by Google. It will probably take a lot less to get an EMD site penalized nowadays; therefore I recommend you look for a brandable domain name instead. Find a domain name that people will remember.

What is a low quality EMD?

I would say that any EMD that is not a brand or company name is at risk of being labeled low quality. The reason is simply that EMDs are chosen by webmasters to rank for a particular phrase.

Webmasters have traditionally looked at their keyword research, found a phrase that is commercially attractive (low competition, high search volume, high AdWords Cost per click) and registered the phrase as an EMD with the intention of ranking for that phrase and monetizing with Google AdSense. Any website that is setup with the primary goal of ranking for a single phrase is likely to be low quality in the eyes of the search engines; after all, websites are there to display quality information on topics, not single phrases.

One thing that makes a lot of these low quality EMDs stand out is the high percentage of backlinks that use the exact same keyword phrase as anchor text. The problem for EMD owners is that using that phrase is natural, because it's the name of the website. This is why I suggest you avoid them, unless it is your company/brand name.

Summary: Any EMD that has obviously been chosen solely for it potential profit is likely to have problems going forward.

Site structure

The way you structure your site is extremely important not only for the search engines but also human visitors. Good organization coupled with a clear and intuitive navigation system is vital.

From a human point of view, it makes sense that content on a similar topic should all be found in the same section of the site. For example, if you have a website selling bicycles, all of the mountain bikes should be found together, all of the road bikes in another section, and maybe bikes for children in another section.

If a 22 year old mountain bike rider came to your site, she should be able to browse the mountain bike stuff without seeing road racers or children's bicycles.

If you're using WordPress as a site builder, organizing your site like this is extremely easy. You simply create a category for each section and assign that category to relevant posts as you publish them. I tend to only assign one category to every post as this makes for a tighter organization (a better silo). If I need to further categorize the articles, e.g. having all 26 inch frame bikes on the same page, I'd use tags instead of categories for the frame sizes. We'll look at tags a little later.

This type of "silo" structure works very well for the search engines as well because it helps them categorize your content. Think of the site that has reviews on the following bikes and accessories.

- Allen Deluxe 4-Bike Hitch Mount Rack

- GMC Denali Pro Road Bike

- GMC Denali Women's Road Bike

- GMC Topkick Dual-Suspension Mountain Bike

- Hollywood Racks E3 Express 3-Bike Trunk Mount Rack

- Kawasaki DX226FS 26-Inch Dual Suspension Mountain Bike

- Mongoose Exile Dual-Suspension Mountain Bike

- Pacific Stratus Men's Mountain Bike

- Topeak Explorer Bike Rack

- Victory Vision Men's Road Bike

If you were to put them into related group (silos), those silos would look something like this.

Silo 1 Mountain Bikes

GMC Topkick Dual-Suspension Mountain Bike

Kawasaki DX226FS 26-Inch Dual Suspension Mountain Bike

Mongoose Exile Dual-Suspension Mountain Bike

Pacific Stratus Men's Mountain Bike

Silo 2 Road Bikes

GMC Denali Pro Road Bike

GMC Denali Women's Road Bike

Victory Vision Men's Road Bike

Silo 3 Car Racks

Allen Deluxe 4-Bike Hitch Mount Rack

Hollywood Racks E3 Express 3-Bike Trunk Mount Rack

Topeak Explorer Bike Rack

So overall then, the structure of our site would be as follows:

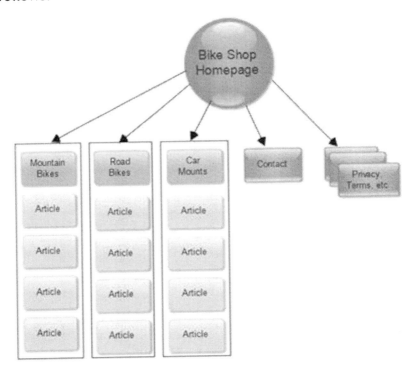

Internal links

One of the most overlooked pieces of the SEO puzzle is internal linking. This not only helps the search engines spider your pages, but it also helps visitors find other related content within your site.

With WordPress, there are plugins that can help you automate some of the internal linking on your site. For example "Yet Another Related Posts" plugin, or YARP to its friends, is a free WordPress plugin that will automatically create a related posts section at the end of every article on your site. You can configure it so that it can only find related posts within the same category if you want and this can help create a tighter, more natural silo with articles linking out to related content on your site.

Here is an example of a "Related Posts" section from a post on one of my own websites:

Related Articles

- Top 12 WordPress Plugins For WordPress 2.7.x - Here is my top 12 V 2.7.x Bookmark on DeliciousDigg this postRecommend on Facebook with StumblersTweet about itBuzz it upSubscribe to the comments on

- Top 10 WordPress Plugins - NOTE: This article is quite old. On 10th with an update of what plugins I use. The article is Top 12 WordPres: WordPress Plugins. I do use others, but these are the first ones I ins WordPress site. 1.

- Best WordPress Ratings & Review Plugin? - WordPress is a fantastic with a ratings and review plugin, your visitors can actually add value tc ratings and reviews of products. I tested out 4 WordPress Ratings & F winner. Bookmark on DeliciousDigg this postRecommend on Facebc

There are a number of "related posts" plugins that you can use to achieve the same thing.

Linking pages together

Another form of internal linking, which I think is extremely important, is links within the body of your articles.

For example, if you are writing an article about the "GMC Topkick Dual-Suspension Mountain Bike", you might like to compare certain features of the bike to the "Mongoose Exile Dual-Suspension Mountain Bike". When you mention the name of the Mongoose Exile bike, it would help your visitors if you linked that phrase to your Mongoose Exile review.

This would also help the search engines to find that article, and help them determine what it is about (based on the link text).

This type of internal linking helps to increase indexing of your site as well as the rankings of individual pages.

To read more about internal linking between pages on your site, I recommend you read an article that I wrote on the subject called "Internal Linking & SEO".

Tags - another way to categorize your content

Tags are another way to categorize content if you are running a WordPress site. When you write a post, you can include a number of these tags which can help further categorize the piece.

For example, if you wrote a post about the "Dyson DC 33 Animal" vacuum, you would probably put it in the category "Dyson" as that is the most logical "navigation label" for your visitors.

However, you might also want to allow visitors to easily find vacuums that use the Dyson Ball technology, or contain a HEPA filter. Rather than have a category for "Dyson Ball" and "HEPA filter" and then put that DC33 animal in all three categories, a better way would be to create tags for this extra classification.

For example, here are some tags you might use on your vacuum site:

• Upright
• Dyson Ball

- Pet hair

- HEPA filter

- Bagless

These tags will help to categorize the posts within the Dyson category (and every other category on your site).

WordPress actually creates a page for each of these tags and each of these tag pages can actually rank quite well in Google.

Let's use look at an example.

These four vacuums all have a HEPA filter:

1. Eureka Boss Smart-Vac Upright.
2. Hoover Windtunnel
3. BISSELL Cleanview Helix Upright Vacuum Cleaner
4. Miele S2 Series Lightweight

The first vacuum will be in the Eureka CATEGORY with all other Eureka vacuums.

The second vacuum will be in the Hoover CATEGORY with all other Hoover vacuums.

The third vacuum will be in the Bissell CATEGORY with all other Bissell vacuums.

The fourth vacuum will be in the Miele CATEGORY with all other Miele vacuums.

However, all 4 vacuums would also appear on the HEPA Filter "tag page".

In addition, the first three would all appear on the

"Upright" tag page with all other upright vacuums.

When people visit your site, they'll be able to narrow down their choice by Brand (using category navigation), or by looking for specific features (using Tags to navigate).

WARNING

I advise that you use tags wisely. Don't tag every post with hundreds of tags. Think about your tags and only include the most relevant ones for each post.

Use and abuse of tags

A lot of people do not really understand the significance of tags, and see them as a "keyword list" much like the "vestigial" keyword Meta tag. To that end, they create long tag lists for each post. Here is a screenshot of some tags assigned to one post I saw:

Tags: advantages disadvantages of solar power, advantages of a solar panels, advantages of solar cell panel, are MONOCRYSTALLINE sollar pannels good, best mono solar panel price, best quality monocrystaline solar panels, bestpv panels mono or poly, buy pv panels monocrystalline, compare monocrystalin policrystalin photovoltaic, compare monocrystalline and polycrystalline, compare monocrystalline and polycrystalline pannel, compare pollycrystalline vs. monocrystaline modules, crystal cells for solar panels, crystal solar, crystalline si solar efficiency, crystalline solar best, crystalline solar cell technology, crystalline solar cells cost, crystalline solar panels, crystalline solar plate cost, crystalline solar pv module, csun mono-crystalline panels, describe 2 advantages of solar cells, difference between mono and polycrystalline, difference between monocrystalline, difference monocrystalline polycrystalline solar, difference solar panels polycrystalline &, disadvantage to many solar panels, ecokes monocrystalline, ecokes photovoltaic panels, ecokes solar panel, electricity, energy, how i get Monocrystalline silicon, how many rating monocrystalline cell, how Monocrystalline cells are made, how to produce monocrytaline silicon, http://www.monocrystal photo cells/, is monocrystalline better than polycrystalline, is monocrystalline PV best, LUXOR Solar Mono Crystal Dickschichtmodule, maker of monocrystalline panels, mon vs poly efficiency, mono and poly crystalline, mono crystalline pv panels, mono or poly solar panels, mono silicon solar panels, mono solar panel dimensions, mono solar power, mono v poly solar panels, mono versus poly crystalling panels, mono vs poly crystalline panels, mono vs. multicrystalline solar panel, Mono-Crystalline & Poly crystalline, mono-crystalline cells vs poly, mono-crystalline efficiency rating, Mono-Crystalline or Polycrystalline solar panel, Mono-crystalline pv solar

They just keep scrolling down the page. What you see in that list is just one QUARTER of the tags listed for that particular post.

In SEO terms, this is bad practice, very bad!

To understand why long tag lists is generally a bad idea, let's look what happens when you create a post.

When you make a post on your blog, WordPress will try to put the post on several pages of your site including:

1. A page specially created to show the post

2. The category page

3. On every tag page

4. On the author page

Can you see how that one post can be duplicated on multiple pages of your site?

Duplicate content on a site is NOT a good thing!

Let's consider now the tag pages that are created when you make a post.

If you have 50 tags assigned to a post, that article will be posted 50+ times on your blog (on 50 different tag pages plus the other pages mentioned above).

Another big problem with using lots of tags occurs when a particular tag is only used for one post. In that case, the tag page will only have the one article on it, meaning it is almost identical to the post page created by WordPress for that article.

How to use WordPress tags properly

Get into the tag mindset!

Before you use a tag on a post, think in terms of a page being created for each tag you use. Your article will appear on each of those tag pages. Is that what you want? Is this tag going to be used on other relevant posts? Never use a tag if it will not be used by several other posts on your site.

With this in mind, here is what I suggest you do:

During the design stages of your site, make a list on a piece of paper of all the tags you want to use on your site (you can add/edit this list as you build out your site, but have a list you can refer to). These will be the most important keywords for the niche, but they should be keywords that are different to the categories you have set up for the site (never use a tag that is also a category name). After all, WordPress will create pages for each category anyway; so think of tags as an "additional" categorization tool at your disposal.

As you create posts on your site, refer to the tag list you wrote down, and use only tags on that list. By all means add new tags over time, but make sure that tags are going to be used more than once. Don't create a tag that will only ever be used on a single post on your site. Also, only use a few of the most relevant tags for each post.

What if my site already has a lot of posts with spammy tags?

Fortunately there are a number of good plugins to help manage tags if you work with WordPress. Just visit the Plugin directory and search for "Simple Tags". That's one that does a good job in allowing you to modify and edit your tass. Use it to clean up your site.

Modifying tag pages?

Quite often you'll find that your tag pages are getting traffic from Google. I have found that the tag pages often rank very well for the chosen tag (as a keyword phrase).

I like to modify my tag pages so that I can add an introductory section to each one. However, this requires some knowledge of templates, which is beyond the scope of this book.

The tag page I end up with has an article/introduction, followed by a list of all related articles (those which have been tagged with that particular tag). This helps make your tag pages unique, but also allows you to add more value to your site.

Used properly, tag pages can work for you. Used without thought, tag pages can increase duplicate content on your site and increase your chances of getting penalized by Google.

3. Authority

Here is a question for you:

What is an Authority Site?

If you go over to the Free Dictionary website and search for authority, there are a lot of different definitions.   This definition is probably most apt with regards to websites:

au·thor·i·ty (ǝ-thôr'ĭ-tē, ǝ-thŏr'-, ô-thôr'-, ô-thŏr'-)
n. pl. **au·thor·i·ties**
    1.
        a. The power to enforce laws, exact obedience, command, determine, or judge.
        b. One that is invested with this power, especially a government or body of government officials: *land titles issued by the civil authority.*
    2. Power assigned to another; authorization: *Deputies were given authority to make arrests.*
    3. A public agency or corporation with administrative powers in a specified field: *a city transit authority.*
    4.
        a. An accepted source of expert information or advice: *a noted authority on birds; a reference book often cited as an authority.*
        b. A quotation or citation from such a source: *biblical authorities for a moral argument.*

So to make your website be seen as an authority site by the search engines, it has to be an **"accepted source of expert information or advice"**.

That obviously starts with creating a well-optimized site filled with fantastic content (the first two pillars of good SEO that we have talked about). However, alone those two pillars are not enough to make your site an authority, because no-one will have heard about you or your great site.

Your site (or your own name if YOU personally want to be the authority) MUST be well-known in your particular niche.

So how do you get well known?

Well that's the easy part - *you need to put your site name and face out there on as many relevant, high quality places as you can, with links pointing back to relevant pages on your site.*

This all comes down to getting backlinks to your site, but it is also the area that can quickly get you penalized, especially if your site is relatively new or doesn't have much authority yet.

There is another aspect of this I want to discuss before we look deeper at back-linking, and that is linking out from your site to authority sites in your niche.

Think about it for a minute.

We are all part of a huge web of interlinked websites. If you were talking about something in your niche, doesn't it make sense that you might make references to other authority sites?

e.g. If a search engine was trying to evaluate your page on the Atkins Diet, don't you think that links to other peoples studies on the diet, as well as medical references, etc. would help make your page more of an authority? Sure it would, as long as your own content was also excellent. It would also help instill confidence in your visitor by giving them more value.

So when you are writing content for your website, don't be afraid to link to other authority sites if they have relevant information. Don't even use NOFOLLOW links, as that just tells the search engine that you:

(a) Don't trust the site you are linking to, or
(b) You are trying to hoard Page Rank to your own site.

I do recommend though that you open these links in a new window so that your visitors are not taken away from your site if they click these links. What you may even decide to do is have a reference section at the end of your content, with active hyperlinks pointing to other authority sites.

In short, link out to other authority sites - but only when it makes sense and you think it will help **your visitor**.

OK, outbound links are sorted.

What about the links coming into your site?

Backlinks to a website are still hugely important in the ranking of a webpage in Google. It's the main reason webmasters build links to their own websites - to help them rank better. However, there is something very important that you need to know about link building. It's not something that most SEO book or courses will tell you, mainly because they want to sell you their link building tools, or get you to buy recommended tools through their affiliate links. It's this:

Google don't want you building links to your site.

In fact, we can probably state it a little more strongly than that.

Google hate you building links to your site.

In fact, let's take it one step further.

If Google find links that you have created to your site, with the sole purpose of helping your site rank better, they will ignore those links at best, or penalise your site at worst.

Google are on the warpath against "webspam" and "link schemes", and that includes links that webmasters build to their own sites to help those sites rank better.

You need to bear this in mind as you build links to your web pages. Also, just because some SEO guru can show you that incoming anchor text rich links help a page rank better today, it does not mean that this "technique" will work tomorrow. A lot of what is taught in books and courses on SEO are dangerous for the long term. What I cover in this book is what I consider to be the best long-term strategy for link building, and one that doesn't look too unnatural to Google.

OK, let's look at the general concept of link building:

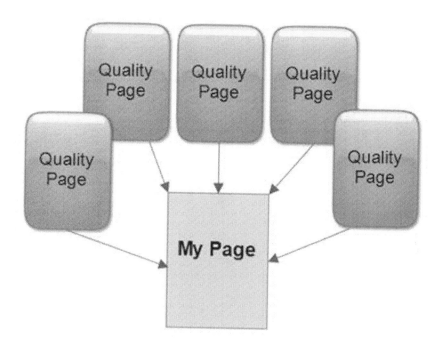

Search Rankings Increase

As you build quality links to your page, your page will move up the search engine rankings.

Some people will tell you that it doesn't matter whether inbound links are on pages which are highly related to your site or not, but that just doesn't make too much sense. And with Penguin and Panda quick to penalize, I recommend you ALWAYS consider quality in every backlink you get. That means quality of the page that your link is on (look to get links on authority sites), and quality of the content on the page your link is on.

NOTE: Having backlinks on pages/sites in a different niche to your own DID once work. However, that has all changed with Panda and Penguin.

Think about it logically.

If you had a website on "breeding goldfish", and you had 100 inbound links to your site but 95% of those were on pages that talked about things like:

- Prescription drugs
- Viagra
- Auto maintenance
- Wedding speeches
- Golf Equipment
- Etc

What is that telling the search engines?

I think that Google would look at these backlinks and decide that you were involved in backlinking strategies with the sole purpose or ranking better. Do you think they'd look favorably at that? No, and their quality guidelines say so.

If the search engines want to use inbound links as a measure of authority, then surely the most authoritative links you could get would be from quality pages that were on a similar topic to the page they link to?

With Google Penguin, this may be even more important as Google appears to be giving less weight to the anchor text and more to the actual THEME of the webpage (or site) that the link is on. Therefore, look for links from pages and sites that are relevant to your own, and look for quality sites to get your links on.

Is Negative SEO real?

Negative SEO is a relatively new term that refers to webmasters/SEOs who build poor quality links to their competitor's website to get it penalized. Many SEOs agree now that since Penguin, negative SEO is a reality. I actually think it was a reality even before Panda.

Before we look at negative SEO, and how it might work, let's look back over the last couple of years.

When Google released the Panda Updates in 2011, a lot of people complained that Google was targeting affiliate sites simply because their site got dropped, or lost serious rankings. My take on this is not that Google hates affiliates, but Google hates poor content and many affiliate sites were poor content. Most affiliate sites I have seen break so many of the Google guidelines that it does not surprise me they got hit. They have poor content and engage in dodgy link schemes.

In the past we all assumed that backlinking could not hurt us. If it could, then a competitor could simply bring your site down by creating lots of spammy backlinks.

I had a site that was several years old and a PR2.

Around the beginning of the 2011 (before Panda) I started some aggressive backlinking. I wanted to use this as a test so I set up about 150 blogs that I could use to get backlinks. I wanted to use blogs that I controlled so I could delete all backlinks if I needed to.

I started submitting content to these 150 sites, with backlinks going back to the pages on my test site.

For several weeks, the rankings climbed, and so did my traffic. I was monitoring 85 keywords, and around 60 had reached the top 10 in Google, with a large proportion in the top 3.

My site then got penalized. All 85 keywords dropped out of the top 100.

They stayed out of the top 100 for 8 weeks. I then started phase two of my test. I deleted all 150 blogs, thereby eliminating all of those spammy backlinks.

Over the next month, things started to improve slowly. Pages started climbing back into the top 100 to the point where I ended up with 64 of the 85 phrases back in the top 100. Around 42 pages were back in the top 30, and 12 were back in the top 10.

NOTE: Obviously my rankings did not return to pre-penalty levels, because they were only at those pre-penalty levels because of the backlinks I had built. However, I think it was fairly clear that my site penalty had been lifted.

So was it coincidence, or did those dodgy, poor quality backlinks really cause my site to be dropped? I have no proof either way, but from what I am hearing, the quality of inbound links may well affect rankings/penalties. This seems totally against what Matt Cutts of Google has told us in the past, but I believe it to be true.

You can read more about this if you are interested by searching Google for "negative SEO".

Let's take a look at how this might work. Here is a diagram:

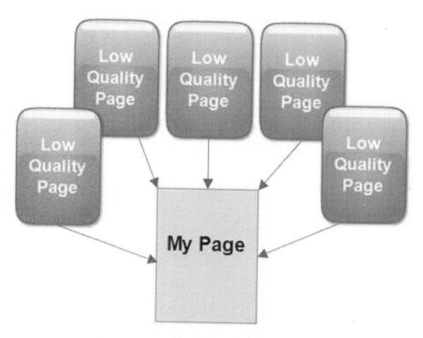

Search Rankings
DECREASE

In this model, poor backlinks actually cause YOUR page to get penalized and drop down the rankings.

We'll revisit this diagram later in the book when we consider the implications of negative SEO to the way we backlink our backlinks.

The point to take home from this is to get backlinks from good authority sites. If possible, get links within the body of a quality article on the page that is linking to you. I realize that is not always possible, but on many sites you can.

What type of backlinks?

First and foremost, go for QUALITY, not quantity.

To be seen as a real authority, your site needs incoming links from other authority sites. Since Google Penguin, I no longer recommend using any type of automated link building tool.

WHAT?????

I know, I know....

"If I cannot use automated link building tools, how can I get enough links to rank well?"

To answer that question, let me ask you one thing.

Do you believe your page DESERVES to rank well based on the **quality of the content** and the **authority of you/your site**?

If you answer no, then you will have to go down the black hat SEO path to get your page ranked, and ultimately that path will lead to penalties and lost rankings.

For a page to rank well on your site, you need to make sure it **deserves** to rank well (in terms of content and your site/author authority).

Think of this example.

You write a page on the "health benefits of vitamin D".

Do you think your page deserves to rank above medical

sites, where the authors are medical doctors? Why? Google clearly wants to show the most useful and accurate information it can to its visitors, and that probably means choosing a medical authority site over yours, even if your content is better. The problem is that you cannot compete on the authority level unless you are an authority on the "health benefits of vitamin D" and that is the way it should be.

How might you gain authority in this area? Well quite simply, you could write articles on vitamin D and have them posted on numerous authority sites, with a link back to your site/page. If you make use of Google's author attribution (it essentially means linking your content to your Google+ profile), which I suggest you do, then Google will know that you have written all these articles on vitamin D, and see you as more of an authority.

When you think about it in these terms, can you understand why I say abandon automated link builders? The links coming into your pages need to be of the utmost quality and professionalism. They need to build your authority, not ruin it by having some computer-generated article with your name on it linking back to your site.

So, with the idea of quality firmly planted in your mind, let me suggest a few places you could get content published that might actually build your reputation and authority. Before I do that though, I would like to give two general guidelines for backlinking.

1. Only look to get links on authority sites in your niche.
2. Try to be EVERYWHERE.

It doesn't matter if your link is on a Page Rank zero page, as long as that page resides on a site that has good authority. Two of the only measures we have of authority are domain age and domain Page Rank, so I suggest you use these. Look for domains that are 5+ years old, with domain Page Rank of 4 or more and you should be safe.

Anchor text?

With Google Penguin, things have changes a lot.

It used to be the case that to optimize a webpage we'd include our main keyword in the page title, URL, H1 header and several times in the content. We'd then point a lot of backlinks to the page using the main keyword phrase as the anchor text.

Google used to reward this type of optimization.

Then came the Penguin, and as we've seen, that type of optimization is more likely to get your page/site penalized.

As well as de-optimizing on-page factors, we have had to de-optimize backlinks to our pages. In fact, if you check out the Google Webmaster Guidelines, you'll see this as an example of a "link scheme":

Links with optimized anchor text in articles or press releases distributed on other sites. For example:
There are many wedding rings on the market. If you want to have a wedding, you will have to pick the best ring. You will also need to buy flowers and a wedding dress.

Google are clearly cracking down on keyword-rich anchor texts in other documents that point to our site. This type of backlinking used to be the norm, but when we look at those links; they really do look spammy, don't they?

Today we need to be smarter about our backlinks. If we want to survive Google Penguin (and all future algorithm updates), then we cannot create backlinks like this. These are the typical types of backlinks created by automated software tools, so that's another compelling reason not to use software to generate backlinks.

I don't believe that Google will penalize all sites that have **some** backlinks like this. I do, however, believe they will penalize sites where the majority of backlinks are like this, and have probably already done so. What I also think is that the number, or percentage of this type of link, that are "safe", and can occur before a penalty results, is decreasing. Over time, Google are becoming less tolerant (and with the disavow tool, they can do this with a clear conscience). Some data suggests that when Penguin was first released, Google did not penalize sites even when 90% of incoming links were spammy. That percentage has decreased so that today, Google probably penalize sites that have 50% or more spammy incoming links. In the months and years to come, there is no reason to believe that Google won't become even more intolerant. How low will this percentage go? That's anybody's guess, but I have personally stopped all keyword-focused anchor text links to my own sites.

Do you have a site where you've done this in the past? Then you need to be careful and try to water this type of link down by getting better, higher authority backlinks. Remove any poor links that you can, and disavow those that you cannot control.

So what is a safe level for this type of keyword-rich anchor text?

Well, I don't believe there is a safe level. It is certainly a moving target. I know you are probably worrying about your inbound anchor text now, so let me go over what I think would be fairly safe limits. We can then look at what I'd suggest going forward with your backlinking.

I would recommend a link profile to pages on your site where:

1. NO MORE than 5% of backlinks use "topical" anchor text. In fact, I'd recommend you no longer use keywords in anchor text from now on.
2. The other 95% of anchor text should be made up of things like the page URL, the page title, the opening H1 header text, and words that are irrelevant to the topic of the article, like "click here", "read this", "read more", "this site", "this blog", "here", etc. The most natural anchor texts to use for any link to a page on your site are the page title or URL. Those are the ones I recommend you use the most. To help build up keyword anchor text links, consider internal site linking, because that is where **keyword-rich anchor text links become natural.**

OK, let's consider that first point. No more than 5% of backlinks using topical anchor text.

"Topical" anchor text links simply means that the anchor text is related to the topic of your article.

E.g. if your article was on "Potential problems during the last trimester of pregnancy", then topical anchor text links would be stuff like:

- High blood pressure in pregnancy

- Gestational diabetes

- Pre-eclampsia

- Excessive bleeding during pregnancy

- Heartburn in pregnancy

- Groin pain in pregnancy

- Backache during pregnancy

- Pregnancy complications

- Complications in pregnancy

- And so on....

This type of link coming in from another website is considered part of a "link scheme" by Google, and will get you into trouble if you have a lot of links like this.

However, this type of topical anchor text is more natural when one page on your site links to another page on the same site (internal site linking), because it clearly helps your visitors find their way around your site. For links you build to your site, I do not recommend using any more keyword rich anchor text. Save that for internal site linking, and link from other sites using the page title or URL of the page you are linking to.

Ranking for a main keyword phrase?

The old way we did SEO was to find out what people searched for, and then optimize pages around those phrases. That way we could rank higher for the phrases people search for, and get traffic to our website. To a large extent, Hummingbird has changed this, though the changes were apparent long before Hummingbird was released. You can see this if you do a Google search. A lot of the pages that rank for any given term do not contain that term in the title. Some don't even include it on the page.

For example, if I search Google for the term **honey bees dying**, only 2 of the top 10 pages include that exact phrase in the title. Most don't even include that phrase in the web page. The reason these pages are ranked highly is not because of the keyword phrases on the page, it because those pages are themed around the topic of "honey bees dying", so include the words and phrases that Google know should be on those pages. For more details on writing content that is themed around a particular topic, go back and read chapter 1.

Backlinking from now on?

I'm sure you are concerned about building incoming links to your pages. What is the best way to proceed?

Well, the good thing is, Google seem to be paying less attention to inbound anchor text and more attention to the topic of the page linking to yours.

For example, if your page is on "Health benefits of curcumin" and you got a link from a page about curcumin or turmeric, then that link would be a valuable one, irrespective of the anchor text used to link to your page.

With that in mind, I'd suggest trying to make your links look as authoritative as possible. Think how academic literature links to another article. They'll use the title of the other article or the bare URL. They might also use the journal name and edition to help find the document. If you were writing a guest post for another website with the intention of linking back to your site, instead of doing this:

Curcumin has shown remarkable anti-cancer properties not only in stripping the cancer cells defenses to make them more visible to the body's natural immune system, but also in cell apoptosis.

.. where **anti-cancer properties** is one of the phrases you want to rank for and links to your site. Do something like this instead:

Curcumin has shown remarkable anti-cancer properties not only in stripping the cancer cells defenses to make them more visible to the body's natural immune system, but in an article "Curcumin initiates cancer cells death", the author describes experimental results showing cell apoptosis occurring.

Do you see how much more this looks like a recommendation to read more information on that topic? Now it looks like something to help the visitor rather than just something used to score points from a search engine? This type of link looks more authoritative, more natural to Google, AND it will be extremely valuable to your site.

If you are submitting articles to other sites for backlinking, then I'd recommend:

1. In-context links like the one above, where the link uses the article title (or URL) and the reader is in no doubt what the destination page is about.
2. A link to a URL or homepage in a resource box, though again, don't use keyword phrases as the anchor text. Use the URL, the domain name or the title of the page you are linking to.

With Penguin, we actually need fewer backlinks to rank well than before, but they need to be from relevant web pages. This isn't just because so many of our competitors were penalized. Google is giving MORE weight to quality links than it used to.

One thing I suggest you do is go after quality links, and then **increase their power** which we'll look at later in the "backlinking the backlinks" section.

OK, where to look for backlinks?

The Best Backlinks

The very best backlinks you can get to your site are the ones you do not create. These are backlinks from other sites, where you did not request the link, nor do you have any say in the anchor text that is used in the link.

These types of backlink are the Holy Grail of backlinks.

They are also the most difficult to get.

The best way of getting this type of link is to develop content that your visitors love, and want to share with others (via their social media channels). Develop content on your site that other site owners will want to link to.

Here are a few ideas:

1. Infographics – these are graphical representations of complex topics. They are very popular items to share on social channels e.g. Pinterest. They are also often re-posted on other sites. When you create and post an infographic on your site, you can include instructions to other webmasters telling them how they can post your infographic on their site (including a link back to your site). You can even include copy & paste code to make things super easy:

2. Scripts & tools that people will bookmark and share. Other webmaster will also link to these. Here is one example of a

tool that searches for nutritional information on a food you
want to search for:

Another good example is a currency convertor script, where
you can convert one currency to another. Or a time zone

convertor. Any tool that you can create, or get created for your site, that people find useful, will attract links from other websites as well as through social sharing.

3. Forums and places people can come to interact with other people in your niche. For example, if you had a website on "Husky dogs", then a forum would attract Husky owners, who would then recommend your site to their friends and through their social channels. Building user participation on your site is a great way to attract natural links, because anyone interacting on your site becomes a potential link builder for you, when they are on other sites or talking to friends.

4. Free downloads like software or PDFs that people find useful. If you can give these away, and people really do find them useful, your URL will be shared with their friends, on forums they frequent and through their social media channels.

5. Posts that include "lists" are the types of posts people love to share on other websites, like forums, in comments on other blogs and via their social channels. For example, "Top 10 Wordpress Plugins" on a site about building websites would be very interesting to people interested in building Wordpress sites. A post like this would get a lot of social shares, plus other sites will link to it. A tip here is to contact the authors of the plugins you recommend, and tell them that they made your top 10 list. Many will link to your post from their site, to prove to their visitors how useful their plugin is.

Use your imagination, and come up with ideas to attract links to your content. These are the most powerful and natural links a site can get, and prove your site's worth to the search engines.

Other backlink sources

This section of the book lists the typical backlink sources recommended by most SEO courses and books. Use these with caution, and I really do recommend you ignore the advice from many SEOs to use keyword rich anchor text.

Article marketing

This is a strange one because some experts believe that article marketing no longer works. I personally believe that it does still work, but, and it's a big but.... don't submit the same article to lots of article directories. A far more productive approach is to pick maybe 10 quality directories and submit a unique article to each one. OK, I hear what you are saying. This means you have to write 10 unique articles. Yes, it does, but if you want to be completely "white hat" about this, and build your authority in a way Google cannot object to, then that is what you need to do. With Google's Panda and now Penguin, this really is the only safe way of doing article marketing. Oh, and don't create backlinks to your own site from within the body of the article. Remember Google's webmaster guidelines?

- Links with optimized anchor text in articles or press releases distributed on other sites. For example:
  There are many wedding rings on the market. If you want to have a wedding, you will have to pick the best ring. You will also need to buy flowers and a wedding dress.

Forum participation

To a lot of Webmasters, the idea of forums is simply to get backlinks from forum profiles. This is something I DO NOT recommend because it easily detected by Google, as is any page that has a backlink to your site with very little content.

Spammers often use software to automatically create hundreds or thousands of profiles on various forums, including a link back to their site in these profiles. This will get your site into trouble. To me it seems obvious that Google can spot this type of linking very easily. Imagine a website with 5000 forum profile backlinks in a matter of days!

When it comes to forums, the best bang for your buck, so to speak, is to get involved in the forum and help people. Make sure you have a Gravatar image (preferably your photo) attached to the e-mail address of your website, and then the same photo on your website. People will see your posts on lots of forums in your niche. You will start appearing wherever they go, and they are then likely to trust you more and click through to your own website. On your website they will see your picture again and this further reinforces your perceived authority. The more they see your photo and read your contributions on these forums, the more they will recognize and respect you as an authority. This is a great way to build authority and it's nothing to do with the backlinks you can get from the forums, though these are useful as well.

Imagine how much of an authority you will be seen as if a visitor goes to several sites (in your niche) and sees you on all of them, answering questions and providing valuable information.

YouTube & other video sites

Creating videos that offer valuable information in your niche is a great way to increase authority and "social proof" (especially if your photo or brand image appears in the video). Videos that you create do not need to be 10 or 15 minute long, you can easily create short two or three minute videos discussing short issues in your niche. Video descriptions can be quite long, and can **include a link back to your site.** If there is a relevant internal page on your site that makes the most sense to link to, do that, otherwise just link to your homepage.

Sites like YouTube give you your own channel which lists all of your videos. Your YouTube profile can even have a link back to your site, and other sites that are part of your network (Twitter, Facebook, etc). If someone sees one video you have done, and they like it, they can then go and check your channel and see other videos that you've created. From here, they can easily sign up for your Tweets or subscribe to your Facebook page too.

There are a lot of other video sharing sites as well, which will also allow you to have a profile page. Try to use the same photo that you have on your site, and that you are using for your Gravatar. We are trying to build up the recognition factor here so that people can automatically recognize you and think "Oh yes I remember him from..."

Twitter

Again we can use twitter to include a brand photo and link back to our main site. As we add tweets, your photo is sent through the system and ends up again in front of people that have subscribed to your twitter feed. Even if you don't have a lot of followers, your twitter page will have links back to your main site, which adds further authority to your persona.

There are a number of WordPress plugins available which automatically send a tweet for each new post published on your site. I wouldn't rely totally on this plug-in for Twitter "content", as it's important to tweet interesting information you find on a day-to-day basis.

Facebook page

Another way that you can increase your authority is by setting up a Facebook page for your site or your business.

Again there are WordPress plugins that can automatically post to your Facebook page whenever you add new content to your site.

Web 2.0 "Blogs"

There are a number of websites that allow you to set up blogs on their domain. Examples include WordPress.com, Blogger.com (owned by Google), Tumblr.com, and LiveJournal etc. You simply go to the site, sign up, and begin posting to your new blog.

As you add more and more content to these blogs, they become more and more powerful (especially if you build backlinks to these blogs).

Since you add the blog content yourself, you can insert links back to your website, but don't overdo it. These blogs should add value and be high quality, just like every other type of backlink we are looking to build. Set up these blogs and post unique information to each of them. That is how I use them. Create small blogs related to your money site, and add in a link to your money site in a small proportion of the posts you make there. Just make sure the information on these "free blogs" is top quality.

RSS feeds

If you use WordPress to build your site, then you have a feed that contains all of the most recent posts (you define how many posts show in the feed within the WordPress Dashboard). You can find the feed by adding "/feed" to the end of your URL (without the quotes obviously).

For example:

http://ezseonews.com/feed/

Once you have your feed URL, you can submit that feed to a number of different RSS Feed websites.

Every time you add new content to your site, the feed is updated, and you get a link back to the new content.

I don't believe that this type of link helps too much with ranking of pages, especially as posts will slide off the bottom of the feed eventually, but it does help to get new content indexed quickly.

I would recommend submitting your feed to only two or three of the highest authority RSS directories that you can find.

I'd also recommend that you set up your feed to only

display excerpts (and a maximum of 10 posts). This should keep you safe from spammers who will try to steal your content by stripping the posts from your feed. Having only 10 posts in the feed is more of a safety precaution as we don't want the last 100 posts hyperlinked on 3 different RSS feed directory sites. This would look a bit too much like we're only doing it to help rankings.

Site directories

Getting your site listed in directories is one of the oldest forms of backlinks. These days, directory listings are not as powerful as they used to be and there are a number of directories you absolutely should not submit your site to.

There are software programs that can submit your site to multiple directories, but I would suggest you save your money and just handpick the most relevant ones (particularly the specialist niche directories that match your chosen niche), and then submit by hand. More is NOT better. Always look for fewer quality submissions where the submission site is a close match to your own. For example, if you have a Paleo diet site, look for directories that specialise in nutrition.

Guest blogging

Guest Blogging is a powerful way to get high quality links back to your site. It's kind of like *Article Marketing 2.0* where you submit articles to sites that accept "guest posts".

The big difference between guest posting and article directories is that guest blogs can be higher quality and much more related to your own niche. For example, you could find a lot of health-related blogs that would accept health related articles from you, but it would be harder to find article directories that were specifically health related.

It works like this:

There are sites out there that are looking for people to write content for them. You write a piece of content and submit it to these sites. If they like your article, they will post it on their website.

When you post your article, you include a resource box that can include links back to your website (or a link in the body of your article). You do need to check the terms and conditions of the sites you are writing for to see whether it's possible to include links within the body of the article. If you can, do that, but make your links look authoritative, like we discussed earlier. Remember, this:

Curcumin has shown remarkable anti-cancer properties not only in stripping the cancer cells defenses to make them more visible to the body's natural immune system, but also in cell apoptosis.

Looks a lot more spammy than this:

Curcumin has shown remarkable anti-cancer properties not only in stripping the cancer cells defenses to make them more visible to the body's natural immune system, but in an article "Curcumin initiates cancer cells death", the author describes experimental results showing cell apoptosis occurring.

The second one is also more Google friendly, as it is not using keyword anchor text. Instead it uses the title of the article being linked to, like a real reference.

Finding Guest Blogs

You can easily find sites that will accept your work by doing a Google search for:

"write for us" + KEYWORD

Where KEYWORD is your main niche word or phrase.

e.g. "write for us" + health

This will return all of the websites that have the phrase "Write for Us" and are related to the health industry. Here are the top few Google results for that term:

86. The **Health** Care Blog
thehealthcareblog.com/
3 hours ago – The Business of **Health** Care ... Last year was a banner year for digital **health**, as the market saw significant growth in ..... **WRITE FOR US** ...

87. **Write for Us** | Help & Info | Her meneutics
www.christianitytoday.com/women/help/about-us/write-for-us.html
Home > Help & Info > **Write for Us** ... parenting, and celibacy, pop culture, **health** and body image, raising girls, and women in the church and parachurch.

NOTE: PageRank data is being displayed in the SERPs using a free plugin for Firefox, called SEO Quake.

With guest blogging, you can pretty much guarantee getting your content onto high PR websites.

These sites can have a lot of authority in the eyes of Google and are therefore excellent places to get your content published. However, there are other benefits too.

Not only do you get backlinks from an authority site, but you'll also get to post your picture and site URL, which only further boosts your own personal authority in the niche. Each article that gets accepted is exposed to a new audience – one that your own site probably never gets. In this way, guest blogging is a great method to "piggy back" on other peoples traffic.

PDF distribution

PDF files (that can contain links to your website) can be distributed to a number of websites. Again, each site you distribute the PDF to can include your profile picture and link back to your site. To create PDFs, you can use existing content or simply write new content for the PDF file.

Microsoft Word or the free OpenOffice suite, both have built in features to convert text documents into PDF format.

One of the best-known examples of a site that you can upload PDF documents to is:

http://www.scribd.com/

You can find a lot of places to submit PDF documents to by searching Google for "submit ebooks".

Again, like everything else, look for quality sites and think less about quantity.

Important: It is important that the backlink profile to your site is diverse! This means lots of different types of backlinks from a wide range of IP addresses.

When to stop backlinking

If you have the link-bait style content we discussed at the beginning of this section, then your pages will attract links naturally, and you should concentrate on adding new, high quality content to keep your visitors happy and attract new links.

If, however, you don't have content that naturally attracts links, you will be doing some backlinking, and I'd recommend you do so on a continuous basis.

As discussed earlier, I'd recommend using the title of the page you are linking to, or its bare URL as the link text.

Avoid using keyword rich anchor text, because there is a real danger of over-optimization as well as Google simply deciding you have too many spammy links and deciding to penalise your site. If you want keyword rich anchor texts pointing to a page on your site, link to it from other pages on your site.

Now, you may ask how you can get to the top 3 for a phrase if you don't build links with keyword rich anchor text. Well, we are back to a point I made earlier. Does your page deserve to be #1? If it does, then by building overall authority to the site and that page in particular, your page will rise to the top, so there is no need to take risks with more anchor text links. Google knows what your page is about. They don't need over-optimized anchor text to tell them. If they think it's worthy of #1, they'll rank it #1. If they don't, then work more on the quality/value of the content, and authority of your site/page. Also bear in mind Google's Hummingbird algorithm update. Pages that are optimized for a keyword phrase (especially commercial keyword phrases) rarely rank well for that phrase.

Backlinks to backlinks

Whenever you build a site you should be tracking a lot of information. One of the most important things to track is the backlinks pointing to your site.

Majestic SEO is a good free tool to do just this.

Once you have set up Majestic SEO, wait for the data to start coming in.

You will get a list of all the backlinks pointing to your site. Download the list (Majestic allow you to download the list as a spreadsheet) and check them to make sure that the backlinks still exist. Delete any links that no longer exist so you only end up with a list of web pages that actively link to your site.

Now, work your way through the list, and point links to each of these backlinks. You can use any method of backlinking you want but I would recommend you only point quality links at these backlinks. This obviously means more work on your behalf, but I'll explain why it's important a little later. The idea is to make each page linking to one of your pages stronger, and therefore able to pass more link juice to your site.

Here it is as a diagram:

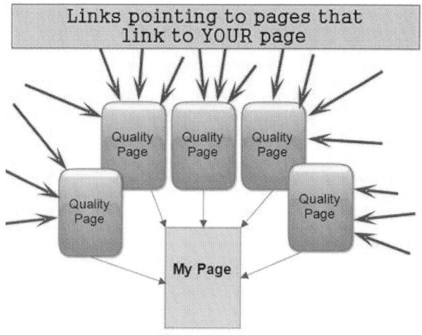

Links pointing to pages that
link to YOUR page

Quality Page

Quality Page

Quality Page

Quality Page

Quality Page

My Page

BIG Increase in Rankings

In my opinion, many webmasters go wrong with this type of backlinks to backlinks. They often tend not worry about the quality of the backlinks to their backlinks. Instead they blast thousands of profile links, social bookmarks, spun articles, etc at their main backlinks in an attempt to boost them.

Most webmasters that use this strategy assume that their site is safe, since these poor quality spammy links DO NOT point at their own site, but at the backlinks to their site (these sites that hold our backlinks are often referred to as buffer sites). They assume that these buffer sites provide a type of immunity against a penalty.

However….. Google hates linking schemes, and pyramid systems like this are no exception. Is it too farfetched to think that the negative SEO we saw earlier could render this type of link pyramid not only useless, but harmful to your site? In the diagram above, if those links to your backlinks are good quality, you have nothing to worry about. However, what if those links pointing at your backlinks are low quality, spammy links? Let's re-draw that diagram.

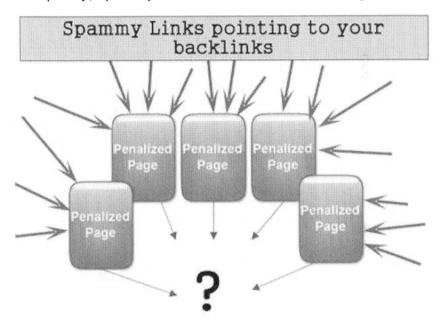

Now, instead of quality links pointing at the backlinks we have poor quality, spammy links, which in turn, penalize the pages that hold your backlinks. What happens now when those pages link to your site?

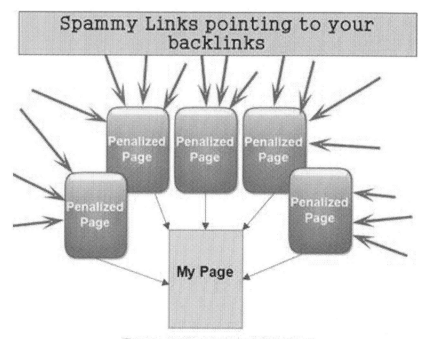

**Page gets a penalty and
loses rankings**

The penalty would be passed down the pyramid, and your pages are penalized. The idea of being immune to a penalty when linking like this disappeared when Google decided to allow links to pass a negative ranking factor.

Could this happen?

A few years ago, everyone assumed that negative SEO was impossible. That is, if you wanted to take out your competition by pointing a lot of poor links at their site, it wouldn't work. Google even told us it wouldn't work. However, with Penguin (and Panda) we know this is no longer true. The truth is, poor quality inbound links can hurt a webpage.

It makes sense though, doesn't it? I mean *if* Google introduced a system where poor links pass on a negative ranking factor, then they would be wasting a massive opportunity to wipe out a lot of spammers if they didn't allow these penalties to trickle down the link pyramids.

So how do we stop someone else building spammy links to our website in an attempt to take out the competition? Well the simple answer is that we cannot. However Google have given us a tool that we can use to fight back.

The Disavow Tool - How to Fix Bad Links to your Site

Several years ago, webmasters were not held responsible for the links pointing to their own sites. Negative SEO just did not work, and Google themselves told us that bad links could not hurt a site's rankings.

In the last year or two, things changed. Google changed the rules so that bad backlinks could hurt page (and site) rankings. However, because of the whole negative SEO angle, Google needed to provide a system where webmasters truly could be held accountable for the links to their sites, whether they had created them or not. In other words, if a website became the target of a negative SEO campaign, Google wanted the webmaster to have the power to fix it. The Disavow tool was born.

The Disavow tool allows webmasters to report bad links pointing at their sites, in the hope that Google will not count them as part of that site's backlink profile.

Therefore, if someone points a lot of spammy links at your

site to try to get your site penalized, you now have a tool that you can use to tell Google about those links, and hopefully get them devalued to the point where they don't contribute to your rankings.

Before we look at the Disavow tool, let me just state something. Just because we can report bad links to Google, does not mean Google will listen or take action. Google have said that webmaster should use the Disavow tool as a last resort. The first step should always be to contact webmasters who are linking to you and ask for links to be removed. If those webmasters refuse to remove links, or ignore your requests, then that is what the Disavow tool is for.

Checking your Link Profile & Creating a Disavow File

The first step in using the Disavow tool is to find the links that point to your site and evaluate them. You need to identify the links that may be causing your site harm. These links include:

1. Those on pages with scraped content.
2. Links on pages with spun content.
3. Links on pages with very poor/limited content (in terms of language, spelling, grammar, etc).
4. Links on sites that have been penalised in Google.
5. Links on irrelevant sites, or sites with dubious content.
6. Site-wide links that appear on all of the pages of a linking website.
7. Any link that you would not want Google to manually inspect.

Fortunately, Google Webmaster Tools provides us with an

easy way to do a link audit. Of course, you need a Webmaster Tools account for this, with your site linked to that account.

Assuming you have had your website linked to your Webmaster Tools account for a while, Google will list the backlinks to your site.

To find these, log in to Webmaster Tools and click on the site you want to inspect.

Now in the menu on the left, select **Links to You Site** from the **Search Traffic** menu.

On the right, you'll see a list of links to your site:

Links to Your Site

Total links
12,787

Who links the most

limesurvey.org	782
blogspot.com	255
topalternate.com	159
similarpages.com	155
youtube.com	145

More »

Google only show you a few by default, but if you look at the bottom of the list, you'll see a link to **More**.

Click it.

You now have a button to **Download latest links.** Clicking this button will allow you to choose the format of the download.

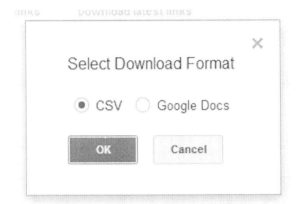

The CSV format will download a spreadsheet you can view in Excel or similar spreadsheet program. Alternatively, you can download in Google Docs format.

If you don't use Google Docs, I recommend you give it a try. Just go to **docs.google.com**

Login to Google Docs with your Gmail address and password.

If you select Google Docs from Webmaster Tools and click the OK button, the spreadsheet opens directly in Google Docs:

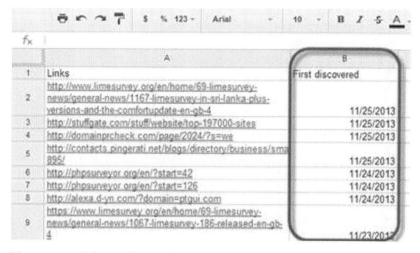

This spreadsheet lists all links Google want you to know that point to your site.

Not only do you get the URL, you also get the date that the link was first discovered. This means you can check all of the links the very first time you do a link audit, and then in a month or two, you only need to check the new links that Google are reporting since your last check.

You need to work your way through the list of links, and pull out any that you really think are harming your website.

Google give you two ways to deal with bad links. You can either report them on a link by link basis, or you can report a whole domain so any links on that domain will be disavowed. You can create a plain text file to use as your disavow list.

To disavow a single URL, just list the URLs, one on each line.

The format for reporting an entire domain is as follows:

Domain:somebaddomain.com

Google also encourage you to use comments in your disavow file. These comments can be for you, or for Google, outlining steps you have carried out to get links removed. For example, if you have tried contacting a webmaster linking to your site, and they have ignored your requests, you can include the comment in your disavow file, before listing the appropriate URLs or domain.

Comments are included by simply using the # symbol. A valid comment would be something like this:

Webmaster has ignored my request to remove these links

If you want to write more, just go onto a second line, with the # at the start. For example:

Webmaster has not replied to my emails requesting link removal

Contacted on 16/08/2013 and again on 06/09/2013

Google provide the following example as a valid disavow file:

In their example, they want two URLs disavowed, plus all links on the shadyseo.com domain.

One you have built up your disavow file, you need to upload it to Google. One thing I recommend you do is to add the following comment to the beginning of your disavow file:

Last updated 10/10/2013

Save the file to your hard disk, so next time you want to do a link audit, you know the date of your last audit and can just look at the new links since that date (remember that Google give us the date a link was found).

Uploading the disavow file to Google is simple.

Go to this URL:

https://www.google.com/webmasters/tools/disavow-links-main

You will need to login using your Webmaster Tools login details (if you are not already logged in).

Select the website from the drop down list, and click the Disavow button:

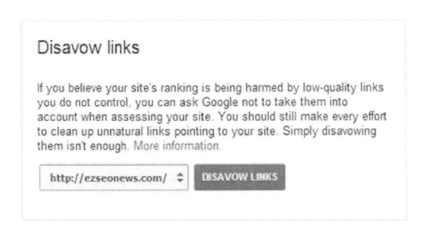

Google

Webmaster Tools

Disavow links

If you believe your site's ranking is being harmed by low-quality links you do not control, you can ask Google not to take them into account when assessing your site. You should still make every effort to clean up unnatural links pointing to your site. Simply disavowing them isn't enough. More information.

http://ezseonews.com/ ⬍   **DISAVOW LINKS**

You will get a warning before you can upload the file you created earlier:

Disavow Links

This is an advanced feature and should only be used with caution. If used incorrectly, this feature can potentially harm your site's performance in Google's search results. We recommend that you only disavow backlinks if you believe that there are a considerable number of spammy, artificial, or low-quality links pointing to your site, and if you are confident that the links are causing issues for you.

Disavow Links

If you want to proceed, click the **Disavow Links** button.

Disavow Links

This is an advanced feature and should only be used with caution. If us potentially harm your site's performance in Google's search results. W disavow backlinks if you believe that there are a considerable number c quality links pointing to your site, and if you are confident that the links

Upload a text file (*.txt) containing **only** the links you want to disavow.

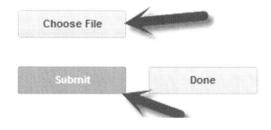

Now you have a button to **Choose File**. Click that and select your disavow text file.

Finally, click the **Submit** button to upload the file to Google.

Updating the Disavow file

When you need to update the disavow file (e.g. to include more URLs or domains), simply add the new URLs and domains to the file, change the comment at the top to the current date so you can keep track, then come back to the disavow tool and re-upload your updated file. Google only keep one file per site, so the last one you upload will be the file they use for any "disavowing".

I'd recommend you do a complete link audit on your site, and then check new links every month or two. Now that you are responsible for all links to your site, you need to know who is linking to your site, and whether those links are potentially harmful to your rankings. If they are, disavow them.

I also want you to think about something else.

If there is a spammy web page linking to you, and you know that it can only be harmful to your rankings, it is possible that the site in question has more than one link to your site, even though you are not aware of them all. In cases like this, I always disavow the whole site rather than just the URLs. If the page on that site is so bad you want to disavow it, then chances are that the whole site is pretty bad.

Summary of Backlinks

I have listed some of my favorite sources of backlinks, though the list is certainly not definitive. There are things like blog commenting and social bookmarking that a lot of people recommend. I wouldn't overdo either of these sources though (or in fact any one source), and always maintain the Quality rule in every backlink you get.

Just remember these simple guidelines. When getting links:

1. Try to get links from as many different places as possible (we want IP diversity).
2. Look for quality rather than quantity. A handful of quality links will do more for your rankings than hundreds or thousands of spammy links (which actually could get your site penalized).
3. Vary your link text. If you have an article on "Flax seeds", check out the Google keyword tool to see what people are searching for when trying to find information on flax seeds. Use these **search phrases** in your link text as well as your **domain name**, **domain URL, the title of the page you are linking to** and even phrases like **"click here"**, or **"this article"**, just to get variation (which seems very important with Google Penguin). I don't recommend you use any one anchor text more than 5% of the time, and instead, **rely on your themed content to tell Google what the page should rank for.** In total, your "optimized links" should not be more than about 30% of all links pointing to a page.
4. Backlink your backlinks to make them stronger, but only backlink using high quality links. By strengthening your backlinks like this, you'll need fewer of them to compete.

5. Carry out a link audit periodically on your site, and disavow any low quality, spammy links that may be affecting your rankings.

4. What's in it for the visitor?

When somebody arrives on your website, you have a very short time to make a first impression. That first impression will decide whether they stay or go, so the first thing you need to do is make sure your site looks good. If you're using WordPress, then that's quite easy because there are a lot of very attractive WordPress designs out there.

Apart from the design, another aspect of your site which will add to that first impression is the speed at which the page loads. This needs to be as fast as possible to avoid having visitors waiting for stuff to load.

Install Google Analytics and get a Google Webmaster Tools account

These tools can give you a huge amount of information on your site and your visitors. They are also Google's way to communicate with YOU! If there is anything Google in concerned about, they'll tell you about it in your Webmaster account. They'll also notify you when your site is down or there is a WordPress upgrade (if you use WordPress).

A lot of webmasters think it's best to avoid these tools as Google will use them against you, but I disagree. Google already has all the data they need on your site, Google Tools are their way of sharing that data with you.

Google's "Webmaster Tools" use to tell you how fast your site was loading and show you a graph of load times over a period of time. However, they have since retired this tool. You can now find that information in Google Analytics though.

A great alternative to checking your site load times is to use an online tool like GTMetrix. You simply enter your page URL and GTMetrix will measure the load speed there and then, in real-time:

Report generated: Fri, Feb 22, 2013, 2:06 AM -0800
Test Server Region: Vancouver, Canada
Using: Firefox 14.0.1, Page Speed 1.12.9.1, YSlow 3.1.4

Looks like you're running WordPress
Have a look at our WP optimization tips »

Summary

Page Speed Grade:		YSlow Grade:		Page load time: 2.63s
(81%),	B	(76%),	C	Total page size: 918KB Total number of requests: 81

Not only do they give you time in seconds for the page load, but they'll tell you which parts of your site are slowing the load time down, and what you can do to fix the problems.

Website stickiness

In Google Analytics, Google will tell you the average time a visitor stays on your site, as well as the bounce rate (how quickly someone bounces back to Google after reaching your site).

Bounce rate and time on site are a measure of how "Sticky" your site is.

Here is the bounce rate for one of my sites over the last month:

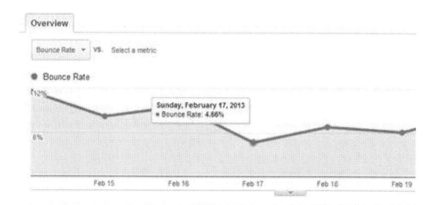

You'll notice that the maximum bounce rate over the last month was around 30%, with the average less than half that. This means that only around 15% of people visiting my site go straight back to Google after reaching the landing page. Here are the averages for this site over the last month:

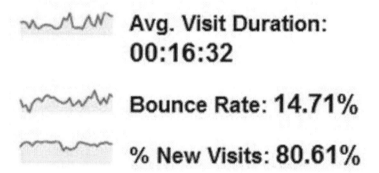

Avg. Visit Duration: 00:16:32

Bounce Rate: 14.71%

% New Visits: 80.61%

Average bounce rate of 14.7% and average time on site of over 16 minutes. I'd say that the site was quite sticky, wouldn't you?

You can examine these metrics for individual pages to see where your site is being let down by any content that does not hold the visitors attention.

The next screenshot shows the data for a number of URLs on my site.

Avg. Visit Duration	% New Visits	Bounce Rate
00:17:10	54.50%	7.75%
01:58:04	42.35%	0.00%
00:27:08	83.72%	9.30%
00:15:53	94.59%	18.92%
00:14:28	79.31%	24.14%
00:06:05	85.19%	11.11%
00:06:47	92.31%	19.23%
00:07:52	92.00%	4.00%
00:05:26	100.00%	29.17%
00:10:51	73.91%	8.70%

Just look for the pages with the lowest "visit duration" and the highest "bounce rate" and see if there is something you can do about them to improve the overall experience on your site. Any page with a high bounce rate is a clear indicator that it is not giving the visitor the "experience" they are looking for.

Important aspects of a web page

You need to capture the visitor's attention and let them know what you have got for them.

In terms of articles on your website, this can mean an eye catching headline that makes them want to read more. If your visitor reads the headline and finds it interesting, they'll then read the first paragraph. The first paragraph is almost as vital as the headline itself, so you might like to try creating an opening paragraph as a summary of what your visitor will find further down the page.

As you write content, try to keep sentences short (20 - 25 words) as well as paragraphs - four or five sentences. People hate large blocks of text, but also hate sentences that are so long they become confusing. When you have finished your content, read it aloud and make sure there are no parts that you have to reread to understand fully, and no parts that you hesitate over as you read them.

To make your article easier to read, use sub-heading and bullet points. Pictures and diagrams can also help break up blocks of text, making it easier for the visitor. It's like that old adage goes; a picture is worth a thousand words.

NOTE: Use ALT tags on images, but do not keyword stuff them. Simply use an ALT tag that describes the image.

Another important point is to use colors and fonts wisely. Don't put white fonts on black background or any other combination that causes eye strain. Black font on white backgrounds is the best, and use fonts that are designed to work online like the Verdana, Trebuchet and Georgia. If you want to see some truly shocking use of colors on the web, search Google images for the term **bad website design**.

While we're talking about content, be aware that <u>people are a lot less patient than they used to be</u>, so be succinct and to the point. Don't waffle just to get the number of words on the page higher.

To make your site sticky, you need to give your visitors what they want. In order to do that you need to know your visitor. Ask yourself:

• Who is it?

• What do they want?

• What answers to they need?

• What do they want to ask me?

If we are talking about your homepage, this should guide them quickly and easily to the various sections of your website that gives them what they want. Your visitor should be able to find what they require swiftly and effortlessly. Needless to say a search box is essential, but that is easy with WordPress ;)

Ways to build Trust

1. A photo of yourself in a prominent position on your website. The sidebars or in the logo are a good place for this. A photo helps build trust because the visitor can see who they are interacting with. The problem for Internet Marketers is that not many want their photos on their niche websites. I would suggest though that the benefits of having a photo

are too strong to ignore.

2. If you use your photo as a <u>Gravatar,</u> then every time you post comments on other sites, your photo will appear. This goes back to what we were saying in the section on building authority. How much more comforting is it for a visitor to arrive on your site and see a face they've seen before on other authority sites? This can really help towards building a high level of trust.

3. Fresh content - If people arrive at your site and see that the content is several years old, this may be enough for them to click the back button. Keep stuff like reviews up to date. If you update a review, change the timestamp of the post in WordPress to reflect the new date. If the content is "ageless", remove the date/time stamp from the post (some knowledge of PHP or WordPress templates is required for this).

4. A clearly visible privacy policy, terms of use and a contact page (and even an About Us page where you can mention who you are and what goals you have for the site), are great ways to help build trust. On your contact page you should ideally have a real address as this helps with the trust building. Again, it's a good idea to have your photo on the contact us page.

5.

Types of content that can give your visitors what they want:

1. Answering real questions – you can find questions that people ask in your niche by looking at Yahoo Answers, Wordtracker's Free Question Tool, Quora and even Ask.com. Find real questions and provide accurate answers.

2. Buyer guides – e.g. if your site is about Android Tablets, give your visitors a free PDF that tells them what they need to know when it comes to buying one. You can use that free guide to build a list if you want, by making visitors opt-in to your list before they are given the download URL.

   Tutorials – Provide helpful tutorials for your visitors if you can think of some that are relevant to your niche.

3. Videos - Create informative, relevant videos and have them embedded in your web pages. Put a great title above the video to make sure your visitor clicks to watch (never have them start automatically – give your visitor the option). Make sure the video content lives up to the title! Upload videos to Youtube.com and develop your own YouTube channel in your chosen niche. This will not only bring traffic, but also build credibility and trust. You can link to this channel from your site.

4. One type of page I usually include on my niche sites is a Terminology page. A niche has its own vocabulary as we have seen, and often people want to know what certain words or phrases mean. You can see an example of this type of page listing on diabetes terminology.

The best advice I can give is to ask you a question.

What valuable information or resources can you offer that are not available on the top 10 pages in Google?

Make your site interactive

1. Allow Comments from visitors at the end of your articles. Invite or encourage your visitors to use the comment box. It's amazing how simple it is to say "Hey, if you've got a question or an opinion on this, leave a comment at the bottom of this post", yet a lot of people don't bother. Darren Rowse wrote a nice article on getting your visitors to comment. A lot of people turn comments off on their blog because of the huge amounts of spam they receive. However, by using a good spam blocker like Akismet (commercial) or Growmap Anti Spambot Plugin, or GASP for short (free), you can eliminate 99% of all spam.

   Comments allow your visitor to interact with YOU (and other commenters) but if they ask a question, make sure you answer it as this starts a dialogue with your target audience and builds trust and authority when visitors see that you're answering their questions personally. Answering questions brings visitors back to your site, especially if you have a plug-in installed that allows them to track responses to their comments. A popular one is "Comment Reply Notification".

2. By using a ratings and review plug-in (search the WordPress plugin directory for one), you can give your visitors the chance to award products their own star rating when they leave a comment.

3. Polls – Allow your visitors to express their opinion by voting. There are free polling scripts available.

4. Provide Social Media Icons after each post so that people can spread the word on your great content. There are a number of free plugins available. Shane Melaugh created a great free one called Social Essentials. It gives you a decent set of options as well as stats on social shares.
5. Add a forum. This can be a lot of work because forums are often spammed heavily, but forums are a great way for people to interact with yourself and others. Several WordPress plugins are available that will add a fully functional forum on your site.

That's it! That's my SEO guide for 2013 and beyond.

So what's next?

For anyone interested in learning my own methods for building authority sites, backlinking and SEO in general, you can join my free internet marketing newsletter.

Finally I want to wish you good luck, and I hope that you enjoyed this book.

Please leave a review on Amazon

If you did (or even if you didn't), PLEASE add a review on the Amazon website. You can find the book listing here:

Amazon US

Amazon UK

You can find this book on other Amazon stores by searching for its ASIN - B0099RKXE8

All the best

Andy Williams

My Other Kindle Books

Wordpress SEO

On-Page SEO for your Wordpress Site

Most websites (including blogs) share certain features that can be controlled and used to help (or hinder, especially with Google Panda & Penguin on the loose) with the on-site SEO. These features include things like the page title, headlines, body text, ALT tags and so on. In this respect, most sites can be treated in a similar manner when we consider on-site SEO.

However, different platforms have their own quirks, and WordPress is no exception. Out-of-the-box WordPress doesn't do itself any SEO favours, and can in fact cause you ranking problems, especially with the potentially huge amount of duplicate content it creates. Other problems include static, site-wide sidebars and footers, automatically generated meta tags, page load speeds, SEO issues with Wordpress themes, poorly constructed navigation, badly designed homepages, potential spam from visitors, etc. The list goes on.

This book shows you how to set up an SEO-friendly Wordpress website, highlighting the problems, and working through them with step-by-step instructions on how to fix them.

By the end of this book, your WordPress site should be well optimized, without being 'over-optimized' (which is itself a contributing factor in Google penalties).

You can find the book on:

Amazon US

Amazon UK

For other Amazon stores, search for **B00ECF70HU**

An SEO Checklist - A step-by-step plan for fixing SEO problems with your web site

A step-by-step plan for fixing SEO problems with your web site

Pre-Panda and pre-Penguin, Google tolerated certain activities. Post-Panda and post-Penguin, they don't. As a result, they are now enforcing their Webmaster Guidelines which is something that SEOs never really believed Google would do! Essentially, Google have became far less tolerant of activities that they see as rank manipulation.

As webmasters, we have been given a choice. Stick to Google's rules, or lose out on free traffic from the world's biggest search engine.

Those that had abused the rules in the past got a massive shock. Their website, which may have been at the top of Google for several years, dropped like a stone. Rankings gone, overnight!

To have any chance of recovery, you MUST clean up that site. However, for most people, trying to untangle the SEO mess that was built up over several years is not always easy.

Where do you start?

That's why this book was written. It provides a step-by-step plan to fix a broken site. This book contains detailed checklists plus an explanation of why those things are important.

The checklists in this book are based on the SEO that I use on a daily basis. It's the SEO I teach my students, and it's the SEO that I know works. For those that embrace the recent changes, SEO has actually become easier as we no longer have to battle against other sites whose SEO was done 24/7 by an automated tool or an army of cheap labor. Those sites have largely been removed, and that levels the playing field.

If you have a site that lost rankings, this book gives you a step-by-step plan and checklist to fix problems that are common causes of ranking penalties.

You can find the book on:

Amazon US

Amazon UK

For other Amazon stores, search for **B00BXFAULK**

Kindle Publishing – Format, Publish & Promote your books on Kindle

Format, Publish & Promote Your Books on Kindle

Dr. Andy Williams

Why Publish on Amazon Kindle?

Kindle publishing has captured the imagination of aspiring writers. Now, more than at any other time in our history, an opportunity is knocking. Getting your books published no longer means sending out hundreds of letters to publishers and agents. It no longer means getting hundreds of rejection letters back. Today, you can write and publish your own books on Amazon Kindle without an agent or publisher.

Is it Really Possible to Make a Good Income as an Indie Author?

The fact that you are reading this book description tells me you are interested in publishing your own material on Kindle. You may have been lured here by promises of quick riches. Well, I have good news and bad. The bad news is that publishing and profiting from Kindle takes work and dedication. Don't just expect to throw up sub-par material and make a killing in sales. You need to produce good stuff to be successful at this. The good news is that you can make a very decent living from writing and publishing on Kindle.

My own success with Kindle Publishing

As I explain at the beginning of this book, I published my first Kindle book in August 2012, yet by December 2012, just 5 months later, I was making what many people consider to be a full time income. As part of my own learning experience, I setup a Facebook page in July 2012 to share my Kindle publishing journey (there is a link to the Facebook page inside this book). On that Facebook page, I shared the details of what I did, problems I needed to overcome, I shared my growing income reports and most of all, I offered help to those who asked for it. What I found was a huge and growing audience for this type of education, and ultimately, that's why I wrote this book.

What's in this Book?

This book covers what I have learned on my journey and what has worked for me. I have included sections to answer the questions I myself asked, as well as those questions people asked me. This book is a complete reference manual for successfully formatting, publishing & promoting your books on Amazon Kindle. There is even a section for non-US publishers because there is stuff you specifically need to know.

I see enormous potential in Kindle Publishing and in 2013, I intend to grow this side of my own business. Kindle publishing has been liberating for me and I am sure it will be for you too.

Amazon US

Amazon UK

For other Amazon stores, search for **B00BEIX34C**

Wordpress For Beginners

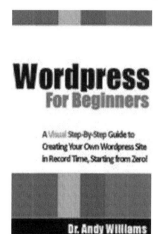

Do you want to build a website but scared it's too difficult?

Building a website was once the domain of computer geeks. Not anymore. Wordpress makes it possible for anyone to create and run a professional looking website.

While Wordpress is an amazing tool, the truth is it does have a steep learning curve, even if you have built websites before. Therefore, the goal of this book is to take anyone, even a complete beginner and get them building a professional looking website. I'll hold your hand, step-by-step, all the way.

As I was planning this book, I made one decision early on. I wanted to use screenshots of everything, so the reader wasn't left looking for something on their screen that I was describing in text. This book has screenshots. I haven't counted them all, but it must be close to 300. These screenshots will help you find the things I am talking about. They'll help you check your settings and options against the screenshot of mine. No more doubt, no more wondering if you have it correct. Look, compare and move on to the next section.

With so many screenshots, you may be worried that the text might be a little on the skimpy side. No need to worry there. I have described in the minutest detail, every step on your journey to a great looking website. In all, this book has over 35,000 words.

This book will cut your learning curve associated with Wordpress.

Every chapter of the book ends with a "Tasks to Complete" section. By completing these tasks, you'll not only become proficient at using Wordpress, you'll become confident & enjoy using Wordpress.

Amazon US

http://www.amazon.com/dp/B009ZVO3H6

Amazon UK

https://www.amazon.co.uk/dp/B009ZVO3H6

For other Amazon stores, search for **B009ZVO3H6**

CSS for Beginners

Learn CSS with detailed instructions, step-by-step screenshots and video tutorials showing CSS in action on real sites

Most websites you visit use cascading style sheets (CSS) for everything from fonts selection & formatting to layout & design. Whether you are building Wordpress sites or traditional HTML websites, this book aims to take the complete beginner to a level where they are comfortable digging into the CSS code and making changes to their own site. This book will show you how to make formatting & layout changes to your own website.

The book covers the following topics:

* Why CSS is important

* Classes, Pseudo Classes, Pseudo Elements & IDs

* The Float property

* Units of Length

* Using DIVs

* Tableless Layouts, including how to create 2-column and 3-column layouts

* The Box Model

* Creating Menus with CSS

* Images & background images

The hands on approach of this book will get YOU building your own Style Sheets. Also included in this book:

* Over 160 screenshots and 20,000 words detailing ever step you need to take

* Full source code for all examples shown.

* Video Tutorials

The video tutorials accompanying this book show you:

* How to investigate the HTML & CSS behind any website.

* How to experiment with your own design in real time, and only make the changes permanent on your site when you are ready.

A basic knowledge of HTML is recommended, although all source code from the book can be downloaded and used as you work through the book

Amazon US

Amazon UK

For other Amazon stores, search for **B00AFV44NS**

More Information from Dr. Andy Williams

If you would like more information, tips, tutorials or advice, there are two resources you might like to consider.

The first is my free weekly newsletter over at ezSEONews.com offering tips, tutorials and advice to online marketers and webmasters. Just sign up and my newsletter plus SEO articles will be delivered to your inbox. I cannot always promise a weekly schedule, but I try ;)

I also run a course over at CreatingFatContent.com, where I build real websites in front of members in "real-time" using my system of SEO.

Made in the USA
Lexington, KY
10 August 2014